TEEN ENTREPRENAIRE

BE PART OF THE NEW RICH AND BECOME A TEEN
MILLIONAIRE ENTREPRENEUR IN TODAY'S
WORLDWIDE ECONOMY

MIKE HOGAN

CONTENTS

INTRODUCTION

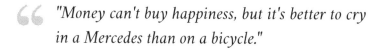 *"Money can't buy happiness, but it's better to cry in a Mercedes than on a bicycle."*

— KENDRICK PERKINS

Have you ever wondered what it would be like to be financially free? To be your own boss and not have to worry about a 9–5 schedule? To live the high life and do what you want to do on your own terms? Maybe you're tired of living according to someone else's rules. Maybe you're nervous about what the future holds financially. Maybe you don't know if going to college and getting into debt is the best option for your financial future. Maybe you've even seen your parents struggle financially and you don't want to experience that in your own adulthood. Whatever the motivation, you're probably enticed by the idea of entrepreneurship and the idea of having complete financial freedom. But how do you achieve this?

You might have dreamed of these things, but you probably imagined that they would happen much later in life for you, or that you would have to wait until your 40s or 50s to start living large. It makes sense, many of the entrepreneurs we see in mainstream media are of a certain age. They pounded the pavement in their youth and then they reaped the rewards later in life. But this isn't so different from the typical narrative of the 9–5 job. You work hard your whole life so that you can (maybe) enjoy some freedom in your golden years. Retiring at 45 is really not that different from retiring at 65—you still have most of your youth behind you. Unfortunately, it seems like even entrepreneurship can leave you in the same hustle cycle as your parents' generation.

Well, luckily for you, there might be a better way. You probably think that you won't be able to start your career until you graduate college, but this couldn't be further from the truth. Even as a teen, you can get a head start on your career and start working toward the financially free high life you've always dreamed of. If you start now, you will be well on your way to retiring early and enjoying the freedom that financial stability can offer you. Through this early start on your journey to entrepreneurship, you could become financially free much earlier in life and actually get to enjoy your youth without the constant grind of a 9–5.

There are many businesses you can start, even while you're still in school. In fact, being a teenager is one of the best stages of life to start a business in. You are relatively financially secure, you have plenty of free time, and you have the drive. Plus, the earlier you start, the earlier you can reap the rewards. You might also have access to untapped opportunities and markets that the adults in your life simply don't. You likely have a stronger connection with youth culture, social media, and the general pulse of the times than adults around you do, and thus, you present a unique and potentially lucrative perspective in the world of business. In short, you're in prime time to get into entrepreneurship, it's all up to you and whether you are able to go out and take it!

In this book, I will be showing you the ins and outs of starting a business as a teen. As a former youth entrepreneur myself, I know all about how to use your teen perspective to your advantage and start cornering markets as soon as possible. The book will be organized into eight chapters that will each deal with a different aspect of the entrepreneurial process. They are all designed to walk you through it in the simplest way possible.

- In the first chapter, I will explain how to gain a solid foundation of financial skills to ensure that you know how to handle your money before you start making it.
- In the second chapter, I will talk about how important it is to do what you love when trying to earn money as an entrepreneur.
- Then, in the subsequent chapter, I will talk about how it is equally important to play to your skills and start a business based on what you're good at.
- After that, I will move on to talking about what your niche is in entrepreneurship and how to find and access that demographic.
- Then, Chapter 5 will get into the meat of things: how to actually start your business in the real world.
- Chapter 6 will then discuss the importance of personal growth and working on yourself throughout the whole entrepreneurship process.
- After that, in Chapter 7, I will spend some time warning you about the potential dangers of

running a business and caution you about some
things that can possibly go wrong.

- And finally, in Chapter 8, I will highlight some
of the best entrepreneur role models in the
world today that you should be looking up to.

By the end of this book, you should be a solid expert in
entrepreneurship, burning with excitement to start
your first business!

1

A FOUNDATION FOR WEALTH AND SUCCESS

" *"Money is a terrible master but an excellent servant."*

— P.T. BARNUM

Before you can become a successful entrepreneur, you need to build a strong foundation for managing your money (once you have it). Making a bunch of money is useless if you don't know how to manage it well. Money can open so many doors for you and lead you to a life of luxury and enjoyment, but at the same time, it can also take control of your life. Not spending properly, not investing, and not putting a limit to your working hours can start to mean that money is controlling your life, rather than the other way around.

Learning proper financial skills will guarantee that once you get your money, you will wield that power properly. If you have ever heard the phrase "make your money work for you," then you will know what I am getting at here. In this chapter, we are going to lead you through a series of basic financial skills that you should develop early on in life so as to have a strong foundation when you build your fortune.

First, I will debunk some of the most common misconceptions people tend to have about money and offer you some solutions. Then, I will pivot into core financial skills, including saving, budgeting, banking, and building a credit rating. And finally, I will talk about some of the best ways to improve your money mindset and your relationship with money. By the end of this chapter, you should be well-equipped for your general financial future.

COMMON MISCONCEPTIONS ABOUT MONEY

We all have misconceptions to do with money. And with money being so prevalent in most people's lives, it's no wonder that this is the case. Many people have a very fraught relationship to money, sometimes due to financial troubles and sometimes due to a negative financial mindset. But this need not be the case. If you are able to get some of these misconceptions out of your head, then you will find yourself a lot happier and —hopefully—richer. Here, we will look at and debunk some of the most common misconceptions people tend to have about money.

Misconception #1: I Don't Deserve Money

If you have particularly low self-esteem, or even grew up without a lot of money, you might have developed a narrative that tells you you don't deserve to have money. You might think that you're not smart, good, or hard working enough to be among the rich. You might even feel that you haven't done enough to earn it. This is similar to the phenomenon of imposter syndrome, wherein the sufferer believes that they haven't actually earned the things they own, assuming they are a kind of "imposter" and that they have tricked everyone into thinking they are a worthwhile person. This can affect new entrepreneurs and successful ones alike.

But this mindset is flawed from both perspectives. From the perspective of the already successful person, it ignores the fact that they have already experienced success in their life and that success must have come from somewhere. People don't get rich by accident—it takes a lot of dedication. Chances are, if you have succeeded, you've done something right. Now, from the perspective of the person who has not yet succeeded, they are making assumptions based on something that hasn't happened yet. If you think you don't deserve money because of your lack of skills, then you haven't given yourself a chance yet. Thus, from both perspectives, this imposter syndrome is categorically false.

This mindset can also have another harmful effect, which is to stop you from trying. If you don't believe you deserve success, then you are going to have less incentive to try for it. But look at it this way: Why not you? What is different about you when compared with all the other people trying to find success in this world? If you believe that you don't deserve success, then you're also saying that anyone who's like you doesn't deserve it either. As we can see, this mindset does nothing for you financially, and it can really bog you down when it comes to your ability to strive. If you feel this way, then remind yourself that you deserve everything that your hard work earns you.

Misconception #2: Money Is Bad for the Soul

We've all read stories or watched films like *A Christmas Carol* or *Citizen Kane*, where we learn the lesson that being miserly is cruel and only leads to tragedy. Or we've heard proverbs like "It's easier for a camel to go through the eye of a needle than for a rich man to go to heaven," but these are all just manifestations of one opinion.

Yes, being stingy with people and exploitative of your workers is wrong, but that isn't the way everyone behaves with their money. In fact, many very wealthy people are using their fortunes for good, choosing to place the majority of their riches in the hands of those who are working to improve the world. Look at people like Bill Gates who has donated so much of his wealth to humanitarian causes. Plus, the higher the tax bracket you are in, the more of your money is going toward the public funding of things like education, roads, and help for the homeless. Through your high tax dollars and charitable efforts, you can actually do a lot for society by being rich. So, if you believe having a lot of money is a negative thing, or that it will lead to mental anguish, just think about how many good things you can do for the world.

Misconception #3: Money Is Meant to Be Spent

In the financial world, there's a phenomenon known as "living to your means." What this essentially describes is that as people's incomes go up, so too does their cost of living. Making a higher salary might make you want to move to a nicer apartment with higher rent, or you might choose to go on more expensive vacations. You might sign up for more subscriptions or buy a nicer car. Before you know it, your higher salary no longer feels higher, and you have the same disposable income as before.

Because you have let your cost of living inflate, you are essentially making the same amount of money as before —and thus the same amount is being saved and invested—albeit in a nicer apartment or car. If you take the mindset that the money in your bank account is supposed to be spent, then you will not get very far. Living below your means, or at least, not letting your income dictate your means, will leave more of that higher salary to be reinvested or saved, rather than frittered away on more superficial pursuits.

Misconception #4: There Will Always Be Enough Money

If you grew up relatively well-off, then you might not be aware of the stakes of your financial decisions. Never having truly run out of money might mean that you don't realize how devastating financial ruin can really be. If you simply assume that you will always have enough money to be able to do the things that you want to do, then you are more likely be careless with your money. You might be more inclined to go into debt (assuming you will be able to pay it off later), or to spend frivolously and not worry about your savings account. These habits can be utterly devastating to your financial situation and can even lead to ruin. So, make sure you are always aware that money can run out at any time and that you are never immune to losing your money. This mindset will help you be more careful and frugal.

Misconception #5: There Will Never Be Enough Money

On the flipside, it is equally toxic to assume that you will never be able to make enough money. This can manifest as the feeling that you will never be able to achieve success, or the belief that you will never feel like you've made "enough" money. Becoming a millionaire might just lead you to want to become a multi-millionaire, then a billionaire, then a multi-billionaire. You might worry that you will never feel a sense of accomplishment because you are always looking toward the next goal, never stopping to congratulate yourself for what you've achieved.

At a certain point, it can start to feel like a never-ending race where your goal post keeps moving each time you get near the finish line. Establishing clear financial goals and making the effort to feel satisfied when you reach them is essential to maintaining mastery over your money and not letting it become your master. At the end of the day, even if you're the richest person in the world, you could always be richer. If you let that torture you, then you will never be happy.

Misconception #6: Money Will Solve All My Problems

On a similar note, some people have the desire to get rich for all the wrong reasons. They think that it will change their lives, make them lovable, or give them better self-esteem. Money can do a lot of things for you, but it won't solve the deeper issues inside. Rich people still get divorced, have problems with their children, and feel inadequate from time to time. There is no way to buy emotional stability. The only way to have a truly fulfilling inner life is to put in the work on yourself so you can develop strong relationships with others and with yourself. If you don't do this, then no amount of money is going to help you feel better. Plus, wanting to become rich to fill an emotional void is not actually a great motivator. It is highly emotional reasoning and might blind you to future opportunities. So, make sure you sort out your priorities, and don't try to make money for emotional reasons.

CORE FINANCIAL SKILLS

Besides the mindset you have around money in general, you should also be thinking about the core skills of managing your money. Anyone who wants to be financially literate, but especially anyone who wants to become an entrepreneur, should be well-versed in these skills. For our purposes, I will be splitting these four financial skill sets up into what I call the four pillars of personal finance: saving, budgeting, banking, and credit. These four pillars will form the building blocks of the way you manage your money throughout your life. You will need to manage all four of them well if you are truly going to be financially successful. In this section, we will go through all four of these skills and offer you key tips on how to maximize them to their fullest potential.

Saving

When it comes to managing money, saving is typically the first thing people learn. You can even start learning important saving skills as a child. Think about the first time you wanted to buy something that was beyond the scope of your weekly allowance. You probably had to put aside a portion of your allowance every week for a few weeks, or even a few months, so that you could buy that thing you wanted.

This skill is essential to early financial literacy. It can help you learn the value of money and also teach you to really refine the things that are important to you in your spending. As you get older, you will start to have more and more things to save for, and thus, you will need to practice saving in a more complex way. This will allow you to go on trips, pay for school, and even purchase properties or start businesses. Here, we will give you some key tips on how to save you money effectively.

Tip #1: Split Your Savings

If you are starting out with a savings account, then you probably have just two bank accounts: your checking and your savings. This is typical and it helps you distinguish your spending money from your saving money. However, this doesn't really do much for the way that you are going to be breaking up your savings. Like I said in the introduction to this section, you will have more and more things you want to save for as you go through life. So, you will want to start creating different savings accounts for different things.

There are two main ways to split your savings. The first is to put them into different kinds of savings accounts that have different interest rates. Since this falls more under the category of banking, I will leave it for the banking section below. The second way to split your savings, which I will talk about here, is to categorize your savings or savings accounts by their purposes. To do this, reflect on the different areas of your life that you want to save for.

Maybe you are interested in traveling, starting a business, and going to college. In this case, you could start four savings accounts, one for your travel budget, one for your entrepreneurial budget, one for your education, and one for emergencies and miscellaneous expenses. The final category is always a good idea, even if you think you have all your bases covered. These categories will help to make sure that you are devoting enough money to all the things that you want to do.

Tip #2: Save by Percentage

The next aspect of saving that you are probably wondering about is how much you should be saving. This is tricky to define, especially if you don't have a good grasp on your expenses. If you are living with your parents and have all your basic needs covered, then you can save and spend on a 50/50 basis. That means 50% of your income can go toward wants and activities, like a video game or a night out at the movies with friends. You deserve to enjoy some of your income. Then, the other 50% can go straight into your savings. However, if you are living on your own and paying for your own necessities, then you should follow the 50/30/20 rule, meaning 50% of your budget should go toward necessities, 30% toward wants, and 20% toward savings. I will talk about this in more depth in the budgeting section. This way, you will have a good amount saved up by the time you want to start your business!

The second part to this percentage method is to combine it with Tip #1. So, if you are saving 50% of your income, say, you will also need to further divide that up into your saving categories. You should determine how much money should go toward each category on an axis of priority to cost. So, say travel is a high priority, but you are planning to go backpacking on a tight budget. Then, you could devote a smaller percentage to travel.

But if starting a business is your top priority, and that costs quite a bit of money, then you should devote a higher percentage to it. In this case, you could have a model that looks like this:

- Total savings: 50% of income
- Travel: 10% of income
- Business: 30% of income

- Misc: 10% of income

This way, you will be able to save enough money to do everything you want to do without having too much going toward one area. Everything gets its fair share.

Tip #3: Sort Out Spending Priorities to Save Money

If you're up with the popular trends in modern financial literacy, you've probably heard a lot about how to cut your spending. One of the most popular pieces of spending advice is to skip buying coffee every day. After all, if you get a $5 latte from a fancy coffee shop every day, that adds up to $150 a month and a whopping $1800 a year! If you invested or saved all that, you could buy a fancy laptop or go on a nice trip. But as staggering as those numbers are, let's talk about what they really mean.

Yes, lattes add up, but they aren't necessarily bad if they are important to your life. For example, if you have a coffee with your friend every day after work at your favorite independent café, which is really important to you, that's actually money you're investing in your relationships. You can then think about that $1800 per year as money well-spent because it helped you to develop your relationship with someone you care about and create a connection to a small business. However, if you like to save an extra five minutes every morning by buying your coffee on your way to work instead of making it at home, that might not be the best use of your money. That $1800 then starts to look like a laziness budget that you could completely eradicate if you just got up five minutes earlier every day. So, when you're thinking of where to cut money and how to put it toward your savings, make sure you are really being honest with yourself about your priorities.

Budgeting

Besides saving your money, you should also think about budgeting and how it should work in your financial life. You can think of saving as a kind of branch off of budgeting, which is the entire picture. When you budget your money, you are essentially creating a plan for how you are going to be spending your money each week. This skill is incredibly important, not just for your personal finance going forward in your life, but also for your business skills as well. If you don't set a precedent for how much you should be spending on each part of your life, it's very easy for things to get out of hand and for you to completely lose control of your spending. People who budget well for themselves budget well for their businesses. In this section, we will give you some important tips for how you can create a successful budget for yourself.

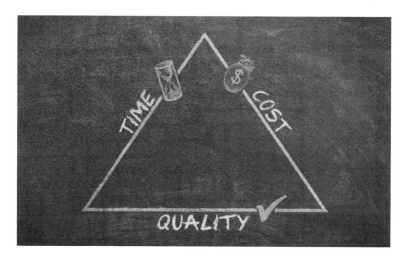

Tip #1: Be Realistic

One of the biggest rookie mistakes that people make with budgeting is being unrealistic about how they spend their money. For example, if you're a person who likes to eat out a lot and that's a big part of your social life, then setting your eating-out budget at $50 isn't going to get you very far. Yes, it's good to try to cut down on spending, but you should still be realistic about what you actually spend, otherwise you are just going to end up breaking your budget.

You can think of budgeting like dieting, kind of, but with money. If you love potato chips and crave them every day, trying to quit them cold turkey is going to set you up for failure. Instead, if you want to cut down on an area of spending, calculate how much you spend on it in an average month and try to cut down by 10%.

So, say you figured out that you spent $200 while eating out last month. Instead of trying to cut that down to ¼ and making it $50, which you will probably find impossible, challenge yourself to get it down to $180. If that goes well, then the next month, challenge yourself to get it down to $150. However, remember, as I said back in the saving section, don't feel like you need to sacrifice aspects of your life that bring you joy. But still, be realistic about your saving goals.

Tip #2: Differentiate Between Higher and Lower Pleasures

In philosophy, there is a distinction between pleasures that are "higher" and pleasures that are "lower." The distinction between these two can be complex, but for the purposes of this book, I will define them as self-improvement pleasures and dopamine pleasures.

Self-improvement pleasures are things that are enjoyable, and they also enrich your life in a meaningful way. These are usually things that educate you in some way, allow you to express yourself creatively, or are physically healthy. So, some examples of higher pleasures would be taking a pottery class, going cycling, or cooking a healthy meal for friends. These are things that take effort but are generally enjoyable and give you a huge payoff in terms of your sense of self.

Lower pleasures, or dopamine pleasures, usually require less effort and have low personal return or even a negative return. These are things that don't enrich you or educate you, and they tend to be things that are unhealthy. Binging TV shows, scrolling through your phone, and eating junk foods are all examples of lower pleasures. When you are budgeting, you should make sure that you set aside more money for higher pleasures than lower ones.

Maybe you could unsubscribe from a streaming service, and instead, use that money to join a weekly yoga class. Maybe you skip the weekly fast-food night and instead use that time and money to learn a new gourmet recipe every week. This is not to say that you should never engage in lower pleasures. After all, who doesn't love the occasional Netflix and pizza night? But in your budgeting, especially for your "wants" budget, try to prioritize wants that enrich you, rather than making you less healthy.

Tip #3: Try 50/30/20 On Your Own Terms

As I mentioned earlier in the savings section, a key piece of budgeting advice involves the 50/30/20 rule, devoting 50% of your budget to necessities, 30% to wants, and 20% to savings. This is great advice and can be the solid foundation of a good budget, but you also need to make it work for you. The best way to do this is to work backwards.

Look at your last month of spending and see what you spent on everything, then see how well it holds up to the 50/30/20 rule. Once you have the reality and the goal in mind, you can start to manipulate your spending to try and get closer to your goal. However, everyone has expenses that might not be accounted for. Living in a major city might mean that you have to spend a bit more on rent. Having a disability or chronic health condition might mean devoting more money to "necessities" to pay for medications or prescriptions. Having an expense like rent covered by living with your parents means you can spend less on necessities and devote more toward savings. All these circumstances will affect the ratio, so make sure that when you are fitting your monthly budget into the 50/30/20 rule, you're doing it on your own terms.

Banking

Moving on from how you are going to be spending your money, let's talk a bit about where you are going to be putting your money. Everyone has to have a bank account, but not all bank accounts are made equal, and there is actually a lot of complexity to this issue. What kind of bank, what kind of account, and whether or not you choose to invest your money will all factor into how you deal with your personal banking. In this section, we will talk about these three main components of banking and how to manage them.

Types of Banks

Did you know there are actually many different kinds of banks? In the old days, you would simply go to the local bank and deposit money, but nowadays, you actually have a lot more options. Let's talk about the two most common types of banks.

The first type of bank is the traditional bank. This is the bank with an in-person branch where you will keep money in a checking or savings account. This type of bank usually has financial advisors, in-person tellers, and fee-free ATMs across your local area. Traditional banks are great if you want all the features a bank can provide. These banks almost always charge a monthly fee for their services, which they will automatically deduct from your account. However, many of these kinds of banks will also have special accounts for teenagers or students so you can get a reduced monthly fee or even have your monthly fee waived.

For the second option, more recently, there are completely digital banks that actually don't have in-person branches at all. These typically have fewer features, but with the advantage of lower or even nonexistent monthly fees. You often won't have any ATM options, meaning you will typically have to pay a fee anytime you want to withdraw cash. This type of bank also likely won't have any in-person tellers or financial advisors. It's the kind of option that's great for the tech-savvy young person who wants to take more control over their finances. However, the choice is completely up to you and your own personal banking needs.

Types of Savings Accounts

Whichever bank you choose to go with will probably have the choice of a few different kinds of savings accounts. These accounts will typically have some kind of interest rate—meaning your money will accumulate just from sitting there—but they are all different. Typically, savings accounts will operate on a spectrum of availability to interest. This means that the more accessible your money is (i.e., you can withdraw it same-day), the lower your interest rate will be. If you want a higher interest rate, then you will need to have an account where your money is less accessible. You might need to wait a few days to a week to withdraw your cash and might even have a limit on how much you can withdraw at a time.

Every bank has a different system, but one of the best ways to manage these types of savings accounts is to have one of each. Put some of your savings in the less accessible, higher-interest account, and then have an emergency fund in the more accessible, lower-interest account. You can think of this like deep storage. For the holiday items you need once a year, you can keep those in shallow storage, but for your grandmother's old tea set that you're never going to use, keep it in deep storage. This is the best way to maximize your savings while still keeping some accessible.

Investing

So, in the last section when I talked about interest in your savings account, you might have been a little confused. *What?* You might have been thinking. *The bank is going to pay me to keep money in there?* It might sound baffling, but this is actually part of the business model of the bank. You aren't actually saving, you're investing. See, banks no longer just place a bunch of cash in the back room and then take it out for you. Your money isn't locked in a drawer somewhere with your name on it. When you have money in the bank, they actually use that money to make investments of their own. So, when you put your money into a high-yield savings account, you are actually investing alongside the bank and reaping the benefits of those investments. Pretty cool, right?

You might also want to make investments for yourself. Back in the old days, you would need to pay close attention to the stock market and make calculated decisions about how to invest your money. But nowadays, investing has become easier than ever. There are many companies that help you to invest your money logically. These are called hedge funds. They are more hands-on than a bank, since you are able to dictate the nature of your investments and see a much higher return. Many of them have a high minimum investment, however, so make sure that you are able to meet this requirement before you invest. This aspect of financial literacy can be done at any age, but it might be easier to do once you've had some success in entrepreneurship and have more money to be able to put into investments.

Credit Ratings

The final aspect of your personal finance that you should be concerned with is your credit score. Essentially, your credit score is a reflection of how well you have handled credit and debt throughout your life. Generally, a credit score of over 700, and especially over 800 is considered very good, while a score of 600 or under is considered not very good.

A credit score can actually be very important, not just to your personal finance but also to your life in general. Your credit score will affect your ability to rent an apartment, get approved for a mortgage, and it can make a big difference in getting a business loan. For this reason, it's very important to make sure that you are always paying your credit card minimums, never bumping up against your credit limit, and not losing track of how much you owe. Credit card debt is a slippery slope and can easily devastate you financially.

You might think the best way to maintain a perfect credit score is to never use your credit card. But the most difficult thing about a credit score is that you actually need to borrow and pay back consistently in order to build up a score. One great strategy is to use your credit card like a debit card, only buy within your means, and pay it off at the end of the month. This way, you will be able to build up credit without getting into any serious debt. Plus, many credit cards have reward systems, meaning you can rack up points or air miles that you can use to buy yourself a treat later! It's a win-win! If you maintain a good credit score, then so many doors will be opened to you, and you will be able to soar financially with no problems.

IMPROVING YOUR MONEY MINDSET

Taking all these skills and misconceptions into account, you're probably wondering about some good strategies to actually improve your mindset surrounding money. Motivation and focus are two of the key components to a healthy and forward-moving mindset around money. In this section, we will give you some clear tips on how to cultivate this positive mindset.

Tip #1: Lean All You Can About Finance

This tip is probably not needed, since you are already doing just that right now! Reading books like this one and pursuing knowledge about business and finance will do wonders for your future as an entrepreneur. You can also pursue knowledge in other ways. Consider watching TV shows like Shark Tank to see how people pitch their businesses to investors and what kinds of mistakes people typically make. You can also find a finance role model, such as a celebrity or a CEO of a company that you admire. Find out what that person did and try to emulate some of their habits and career beats. The more you know about your field, the more you will be able to find success.

Tip #2: Know Your Goals

Before you set out on your journey of entrepreneurship, it's important to have an endgame in mind. Is your endgame financial freedom? Is it being the CEO of a successful company? Is it changing the world with an innovative idea? These are all great goals, but you need to be sure that you are aiming for the one that is right for you.

Try to imagine what your life looks like in 10 years, then 20, then in your golden years. What are you doing? What kind of impact have you made? These kinds of vision exercises will help you determine where exactly you want to go with your entrepreneurial plan. Once you have this vision in mind, then you will have a much stronger aim for your goals. You will have a clear picture of what exactly you are working toward, which is a great motivator.

Tip #3: Create a Charity Plan

There's nothing like giving back. Another great motivator to get going with your business can be giving
back to others. Think of a cause you're really passionate
about. Maybe it's the planet, or endangered animals, or
world poverty. Whatever it is, make sure it's a cause
that makes you really passionate. Then, decide that you
are going to donate a certain percentage of your profits
to that cause. Or, that you are going to donate a lump
sum when you reach a certain income bracket. Or even
that you are going to start a charity of your own with
the money you make from your business. This will give
you an external motivator. Instead of earning that
money just for yourself, you're also doing it for a good
cause. This can really work to motivate you and change
your attitudes toward money to be more positive.

2

DO WHAT YOU LOVE

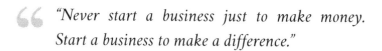 *"Never start a business just to make money. Start a business to make a difference."*

— MARIE FORLEO

Now that we've got the main financial skills out of the way, it's time to start talking about the actual business you are going to start. The first thing you need to worry about when starting a business is, well, what your business is going to be. You might know you want to be an entrepreneur, but you're still not completely sure what you want to do with your business. Believe it or not, this can actually be one of the biggest make-or-break decisions of your career.

Knowing what your business is really about and finding your passion at the heart of it is instrumental to being a successful entrepreneur. It will help you to focus yourself and to give your business the energy and care it deserves. In this chapter, we will lead you through the process of finding the core of your business to decide where to focus it. We will do this by leading you through a series of steps that will help you to pin down the passion that is driving your entrepreneurial motivation.

First, we will talk about the advantages to starting a business in the first place, to give you some ideas about the benefits that might be coming your way. Then, we will look at why having a passion for what you do is important to your business's success. After that, we will give you some strategies for figuring out just what that passion actually is. And finally, we will discuss how to turn that passion into an actual profession. When you're finished this chapter, you should have a much stronger sense of your passions and how they relate to your future in business.

WHY START A BUSINESS?

So, why exactly should you start a business anyway? What are the real benefits to becoming an entrepreneur versus simply working at a job? It's certainly a different lifestyle and one that comes with more potential risks. But it's also a life that's full of intrigue, opportunity, and infinite growth. There are so many reasons that becoming an entrepreneur could potentially be one of the best decisions you'll ever make. Here, we will look at some reasons to explain why starting your own business is an amazing idea.

Reason #1: You're in the Driver's Seat

If you've ever worked a job, you will know how frustrating it can be when you just don't get along with your boss. Even having a boss, period, can be annoying. Someone who tells you what to do and how to dress, someone to reprimand you for being late; it's not great. But with your own business, you can do what's called "being your own boss." You decide how your workplace culture goes and what your hours are. You determine who works for you and what they do. And most of all: You determine what the business is and where it goes. Everything is up to you. This can be scary, but also exhilarating. You are in complete control and can make your work life exactly what you want it to be. This is something that no employee gets to feel, and it can be one of the most liberating things you will experience in your professional life.

Reason #2: You Will Learn a Huge Range of Skills

Think about a large, multinational corporation and how many departments they employ. They probably have an IT department, a marketing department, an accounting department, a sales department, the list goes on. All these skills are inherent to the running of a business but guess what: When you are starting out as an entrepreneur, you will actually have to fulfill all these roles yourself. You will have to act as a marketer, web developer, accountant, and fulfill all those other roles on your own. Again, this might sound scary, but what it actually does is allow you to cross-train and become a sort of jack-of-all-trades. By the time you are able to hire people, you will have a solid grasp on every single aspect of the business. You'll be able to train your own employees and troubleshoot problems much better.

Reason #3: Unlimited Earning Potential

If you go into a field where you make a salary, then there is always going to be a ceiling on how much you can make. Yes, you will be able to ask for raises and move up in the companies that you work for, but there is always going to be a limit to how much you can make in that field. Being an entrepreneur, you can write your own salary, and as long as your company keeps growing, your salary keeps growing. For this reason, there is virtually no end to the earnings you can make as an entrepreneur, setting you up for financial freedom and prosperity.

Reason #4: Make a Difference

When you're working for someone else, it's easy to start feeling like a cog in the machine. You might even be working for a company that goes against your values, or that you feel isn't improving society at all. In these situations, it's easy to feel powerless, or that you're wasting your life. If you get into this kind of work environment, you will probably not be pursuing your personal goals or trying to make the world a better place. To the contrary, if you run your own business, you can streamline it toward things that really matter to you. Maybe that's solving a common problem in people's lives, or providing a service to underrepresented people, or even donating part of your profits to a charity. Either way, you can choose the impact your work has on the world at large, which is a great privilege and pleasure. So, starting your own business can really impact the effect you have on the world and allow you more control.

Reason #5: Improve Your Self-Regulation Skills

Despite it being a great decision, starting your own business isn't for the faint of heart. Or, at least, not for the disorganized at heart. You won't be able to slack off and let someone else do all the work. You won't even be able to forget important details when you run your own business. You will need excellent time management, self-regulation, and organizational skills to successfully start your own business. If you don't have these things, then you are going to fall flat.

The reason for this is that you don't have anyone telling you what to do, which can be both a blessing and a curse. On one hand, you can choose exactly what to do. But on the other hand, it's completely on you to have enough self-control to be able to put the work in. If you are a very disciplined person who has no problem making yourself work, then you shouldn't have any issues, but if you struggle to stay on task when you don't have a strict deadline or a boss breathing down your neck, you might have some difficulties. In this case, building a business can separate the wheat from the chaff and help people who might not be so self-disciplined develop stronger discipline skills. In other words, if you start a business, you will be doing wonders for your self-regulation.

WHY DOES PASSION MATTER?

Now that you know *why* you should start a business, you are probably wondering where the idea of passion comes in. What is the purpose of including your personal interests and convictions in your business? Well, if you can believe it, there's actually a lot of reasons why that can be beneficial. Helping people or pursuing your passions while running a business doesn't have to be a distraction. In fact, it can actually make your business more successful than you ever thought possible. How, you might ask? Well, in this next section, we will give you some concrete ways that your passions can actually lead to higher motivation, truer dedication, and deeper purpose in your business.

Reason #1: Personal Fulfillment

Purely from a personal perspective, doing what you love is simply more fulfilling. These days, many people work in jobs they find uninteresting or even soul-crushing. These are jobs that are not in their field of interest, or they're jobs that feature tasks that are very monotonous. They could even be jobs at companies that are harming the world.

If you start your own business, you have the option to make your work as exciting as possible. So, why not choose a field that you actually find interesting or important? You might be tempted to go with trends or follow where you think the money is, but this would be a mistake. It won't necessarily lead you to greater financial success, and you will find yourself working in a field that you don't care about. At the end of the day, if that's what you end up with, you might as well just get a salaried job. The basic question is: If you're going to start a business, why not do it around something you love?

Reason #2: Motivation

Running a business is hard work. It takes many hours a week—more than the average full-time job—and a lot of dedication. Even the most dedicated person in the world has the potential to experience burnout or fatigue, or even lose interest. However, you are significantly less likely to lose interest in your business if you also have a stake in the actual subject matter. Working for the sake or working is all very well, but if you actually love what you do, you will be able to sustain your interest for much longer than if you are only working to make money. You might even find that you're enjoying yourself, that it doesn't really feel like you are working at all. This relationship to your business is actually a lot more sustainable than simply motivating yourself financially. Doing what you love can help you maintain a close and healthy relationship to your business without experiencing the same degree of burnout.

Reason #3: Inspiring Others

Have you ever taken a class where the teacher or professor seemed uninterested in the subject matter? It can be one of the most boring and unmotivating experiences. They don't go off on tangents about interesting facts or seem to speak with any passion. Instead, they seem to be teaching from the textbook with no real regard for knowledge. In contrast, have you ever taken a class with a teacher who seemed wildly interested in the subject matter? They are much more fascinating to listen to. They have a personal stake in the subject and seem to care more about whether their students actually get it, prompting them to put more stock into their teaching method. The difference here is palpable and can really make or break a student's enthusiasm, and thus, their success in the course.

Well, this is exactly the same with businesses. When you are an entrepreneur, you will need to train employees and pitch your business to many people. If you aren't personally interested in the subject matter of your business, those pitches are going to come across like a lecture from an undermotivated teacher. But if you do have passion attached to the subject matter, then you will be able to inspire others much more easily. People will be more drawn to your pitches, and thus, they will be more likely to want to invest in you, become a client, or even work for you. Your business will automatically become more successful.

Reason #4: You're More Likely to Be Good at It

The reality is, we gravitate toward the things we're interested in more than the things we aren't. Chances are, this thing that you're really passionate about has taken up a lot of your time and mental energy. Maybe it's a sport or an instrument you've played since you were a kid. It could be a humanitarian issue you've read books about, or a specific skill you've spent years developing. If you center your business around something you already know a lot about and have experience with, then you will have already done a lot of the work. Research, especially market research, comprises a large part of the early stages of a business. But if you base your business around something you already know about, you will have a head start on that research. Thus, designing your business around your passions is an excellent way to actually give yourself a leg up.

HOW TO DISCOVER YOUR PASSION

Let's face it: As a young person, you probably haven't discovered everything about yourself yet. Everyone goes at a different pace when it comes to knowing themselves. Some people discover their passions early, while some people don't start until much later in life. For example, Picasso began formal art training at the age of 7, while Van Gogh didn't start painting until he was 27. Maybe you already have a strong passion, be it an area of study or a humanitarian cause, or maybe you still don't know where you will focus. If you are in the latter camp, don't worry. You have plenty of time to figure out your passions. But it doesn't hurt to give yourself a little push and try to dig deeper into yourself to discover the things that really motivate you. In this section, we will give you some food for thought to help you start to figure out your passions.

Method #1: Create a Vision Board

Visualization is one of the most important aspects of creating goals for yourself. Sometimes, you don't actually know what you like until you've seen it laid out. Have you ever planned a trip to a city, loving how it looks in pictures, but then when you get there, it just has a different feeling than you expected? Or conversely, have you ever had to go to a city that you've never really been interested in, but then absolutely fell in love with it while you were there? This is because sometimes we need more tangible experiences with something before we really get to know it. So, if you're a person who struggles with setting goals, consider creating a vision board for yourself.

What is a vision board? Well, a vision board is essentially a collage of pictures that you think best represents your goal. A person might make one to plan for their wedding or decorate a new home using images from magazines or the internet that fit the aesthetic they want to achieve. But you can do this for more than just decoration. You can also create a vision board for your life in general. Find some images or words that resonate with you in terms of your future life. It could be a car you want to buy, a word you want people to describe you with, or even the kind of office environment you want to create. All these things can help you to start figuring out what kind of business you want to have and what kind of culture and impact you want it to make.

Method #2: Write a Profile on Your Future Self

Some people also call this writing your obituary, but this is a less morbid version. If you want to determine what you really want to do with your life, try to envision your perfect future. One of the best ways to do this is to write a magazine profile, in the third person, about yourself at age 30, 40, or even 70. What kinds of things have you achieved? What kind of impact have you made? Are you heralded as a visionary? An altruist? A hard worker? What are the kinds of words you would want to be used in such a profile? How would you like to be remembered?

This exercise is particularly useful for cutting to the chase. We can get so lost in the little everyday concerns of our lives that we hardly have time to consider the bigger picture. This method helps you to really take a grander look at your life and determine, once and for all, the kinds of long-term goals you want to achieve. From there, you can start to really tease out your passions and values in the short term and streamline your pursuits.

Method #3: Adopt a Growth Mindset

One of the biggest mistakes people can make is to close themselves off to opportunities. You might assume that there are a fixed number of things that you enjoy or that you are good at. Thus, you don't seek out new things or incorporate them into your vision of the future. But this is a big mistake. It's called a "fixed mindset." People with fixed mindsets don't leave them-selves very much opportunity for growth because they believe that they have achieved all they can, and that there's no further capacity for them to learn or change. In contrast, there is something called a "growth mind-set," which acknowledges that the human mind is highly adaptable and can change to fit a number of different situations.

With a growth mindset, you could potentially become more interested in anything. So, for example, a person with a fixed mindset might say something like "I've never been very good at writing, so I don't think it's something I'm going to ever be good at." Whereas a person with a growth mindset might say something like "I haven't given writing much attention yet, but I'm sure if I'm persistent, I will be able to improve."

The important thing about the growth mindset is that it doesn't try to pretend that you are interested in or good at things you aren't, but still acknowledges that hard work is all it takes to make something a skill. This mindset is far more productive, especially if you are exploring potential passions. Denying yourself access to a subject because it doesn't fit your narrative about yourself is very limiting, and so, adopting a growth mindset will help you be open to all the possibilities that are out there for you.

Method #4: Find Inspirational People

You've heard the phrase: "You have to see it to be it." This sentiment illustrates how having positive role models can really influence the way that you see the world and yourself. Not having strong role models can make the future seem aimless. You might not believe that your dreams are possible because you haven't seen anyone achieve the kinds of things that you want to achieve. Thus, to be able to really start envisioning your passions, finding someone who has done the kind of things you want to do can be really inspirational. It's best if they also come from a similar background to yours. So, if you don't come from money, or maybe you are part of a marginalized group, you can see that it is still possible to defy the odds and succeed.

Do some research into other entrepreneurs and find the ones that resonate with you. Notice things about them. Do they have a really charismatic personality? Did they start a business in a field that you are interested in? Are they an amazing public speaker? Find the parts of them that you really admire and seek to emulate them in your own life. If they have any kind of media, like a TED talk, or a Masterclass, consider watching it and taking notes. You can also look for role models in your personal life. They don't have to be entrepreneurs, but maybe they're really hard workers or they've overcome some major adversity in their lives. These people can give you the vision, the courage, and the motivation to discover and pursue your own passions.

TURNING THAT PASSION INTO INCOME

So, you've discovered your passion. What now? How can you actually fuse this passion with your business? What are the ways you can incorporate these passions into your entrepreneurial goals? Well, it might not always be easy, but you will almost certainly be able to find some way of turning these passions into something that you can make money from. In this section, we will look at how exactly you can turn your hobbies and passions into lucrative businesses.

Step 1: Build the Skill

Depending on what kind of hobby you are trying to monetize, you will potentially need to have a solid skill set first. So, for example, say you want to start a knitting business where you sell your handmade sweaters and mittens. In this case, you will need to make sure you are a very good knitter. Do some practice pieces first to ensure that you know how to do it well. Maybe make one of everything in each color, a scarf, a hat, a sweater, and then decide if it's for you. You should also try replicating these things on the scale you would need to produce for a sustainable business. So, say you need to make five sweaters a week (or one a day, for a typical 5-day-per-week schedule) to make enough to live on. You should do a trial week where you try to actually make a sweater a day to see if your business is sustainable. Of course, you will get faster over time and might even be able to hire some people to share the work with you, but your business should still be sustainable.

Step 2: Figure Out Your Hourly Rate

One of the biggest mistakes young CEOs make is not paying themselves. They would rather put all their money back into the business. While this might be better for growth in the long run, it also means that you won't get a chance to actually make money early on, especially if you are covering any of your own expenses. But paying yourself also means figuring out how much you are actually making in an hour.

There are two parts to this: your revenue and your profits. Remember the sweaters? More than just figuring out how many you *can* make in a week, you also have to figure out how long they take to make and how much that works out to per hour. The way it works is this: Consider the time you take to make the sweater and how much you sell it for. So, if you are selling the sweaters for $100 each, and each one takes you 5 hours to make, that means you are profiting $20 an hour. That's how much the business is making in an hour.

However, you also have to subtract any expenses. That involves the price of the materials, the space if you are renting it, and any advertising. So, say the wool for a sweater costs $10, the space for 5 hours is $25, and you are spending about $5 per day for an online advertisement. Suddenly, the overall revenue for one sweater is no longer $100 because when you subtract $10, and $25, and $5, you're left with $60. Now you're only making $12 an hour in actual profits, which can go toward your living expenses. If you are going to have a profitable business, you have to make sure that you are earning a decent wage per hour before you go in.

Step 3: Connect With Others Who Share Your Passions

There's no such thing as a successful business without customers! One of the best ways to develop a customer base is to really connect with people who share your passions and form a community. We will talk a bit more deeply in Chapter 4 about how to build this niche, but for now we will just talk about how to find like-minded people. Say you want to build a knitting business. You could try joining a knitting club or getting a part-time job at a knitting store. These places will offer you an in with potential customers, but also with potential distributors and coworkers. If you meet some other amazing knitters, they might want to get in on your business and work for you, or at least spread the word to potential customers. Building community will strengthen your connections in the world you want to start a business in, and thus, widen your network.

3

DO WHAT YOU'RE GOOD AT

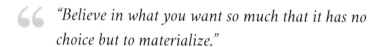 *"Believe in what you want so much that it has no choice but to materialize."*

— DR. JOE VITALE

Along with doing what you are passionate about, you also need to think about the business side of things. Do what you're good at and what is profitable. After all, having a business is about making money at the end of the day, so you have to make sure that you fuse what you love with what can make you money. The good news is that there are a lot of great ways of doing this. Getting a better sense of not just what you love to do, but what you are actually good at is crucial. This will help you be realistic about your goals and actually start playing to your strengths. In this chapter, I will teach you all about playing to these strengths and trying to gain more control over the future of your business.

First, we will talk about the importance of understanding yourself. After all, part of what you're selling is you, so you should know yourself, right? Then, we will talk more specifically about the process of discovering your strengths and weaknesses. In that section, we will also discuss the difference between hard and soft skills, as well as the value of being aware of even your greatest shortcomings. By the end of this chapter, you should be well aware of your strongest qualities and how to steer your business toward them.

UNDERSTANDING YOURSELF

You might think you understand yourself, but you probably don't. As a teen, one of your biggest struggles is discovering who you are. You've probably gone through a few different phases, so far, in your life. Maybe you had a year where you dressed a certain way or listened to a certain type of music. Or maybe you hung out with a certain friend group, but then found that you stopped connecting with them after a while. These things are totally normal and important to your growth and development. But with your business, you

TEEN ENTREPRENAIRE | 61

are going to need to be a little more deliberate in terms of understanding who you are, where your connections lie, and what your strengths are. Let's list some of the reasons you should get to know yourself a little better.

Reason #1: Self-Acceptance

More than anything else, knowing yourself better means that you will have more to feel good about! The more you discover the things you are good at, the more you have to be proud of. In your journey of self-discovery, you might uncover all sorts of amazing talents you never knew you had. You might be able to see yourself in a whole new light, figuring out what is interesting to you and how you might be important to the world. In this sense, knowing yourself can lead to a whole new world of potential for your self-esteem.

Reason #2: Self-Improvement

Not all your discoveries about yourself will be good. No one is perfect, and we all have room for improvement within ourselves. The problem lies in not knowing what you need to improve about yourself. Have you ever met someone who had a glaring flaw that they were completely unaware of? It can get really annoying. The value of knowing your weaknesses, then, is to be able to work hard to counteract them. Being aware is the first step toward self-improvement, and so, you can do a lot for yourself just by learning about what you're not so good at.

Reason #3: Insight

More than anything, knowing yourself helps you understand your actions better. If you sometimes find yourself baffled at why you did something or at why you keep repeating the same patterns in your life, then chances are, you need to do a bit of soul searching. If you learn more about who you are and what makes you tick, then you can have much stronger insight into your reactions and the kinds of things you might do. This can help you a lot both in business and in life.

Reason #4: Develop Your Personal Brand

And finally, knowing who you are can actually help you market yourself better. Every great CEO has a trademark brand. For Elon Musk, it's being an innovator, for Bill Gates, it's being a philanthropist. Finding out who you really are can help guide you toward the persona brand you want to have for yourself and your business. Like I said, part of what you are selling with your business is you, and so you will need to know who that is.

Sometimes, digging deep can help us present ourselves better on the surface. Discovering your innermost personality and values will, thus, help you steer the ship toward who you eventually want to be as a CEO.

YOUR STRENGTHS AND WEAKNESSES

If you've ever had a job interview, you've probably been asked what your biggest strengths and weaknesses are. This is a notoriously tricky question, not just because you don't want to reveal weaknesses to prospective employers, but also because you don't necessarily know what they are right away. No one has a full laundry list of strengths and weaknesses playing out perfectly in their head. We all live in a sort of muddled state, not entirely sure where we stand in terms of our skill sets. Furthermore, there are so many different types of skills that it is impossible to know exactly where you stand with all of them. But all of that can change. Digging deep and gaining more insight into your strengths and weaknesses is one of the best ways that you can improve yourself personally and professionally. In this section, I will lead you through both the benefits and the methods with which you can start learning all about your individual strengths and weaknesses.

Hard Skills vs. Soft Skills

Before we get into strengths and weaknesses, we have to define what areas, exactly, you can be strong or weak in. As you definitely know already, there are many different types of skills. There are social skills, academic skills, physical skills, professional skills, the list goes on. Knowing what these skills really entail is essential for you to be able to map your abilities onto them. Though there are many different versions of these skills, for the purposes of this book, we will only look at two distinct types: hard skills and soft skills. This distinction is very important because it will help you define the different types of skills you have in life and business. Here, we will look at the distinction between hard and soft skills so you can start thinking about the kinds of skills you have in each area.

Hard Skills

If you have ever taken a course or learned how to do something really specific, then you have a hard skill. An example of a hard skill would be knowing how to play the violin, change a tire, or create a spreadsheet in Excel. Anything that has a concrete answer for whether you know it or not, and that you could be tested on. These are excellent skills to put on your resume because you can easily prove them, and often, they are skills that not everyone has. Usually, most people are aware of the hard skills they have. They can be in any area. They can be the ability to make an omelet, drive a car, or speak another language. If you are getting ready to start a business, then you should make a list of these hard skills to see where many of your strengths lie.

Soft Skills

On the other side, we have soft skills. Soft skills are important, but they may be harder to measure and are usually learned from experience, rather than schooling. Social skills, such as the ability to talk to strangers or maintain relationships, are the best examples of soft skills. You might also have really good time-management skills, or you might be a great salesperson. These things can't really be *tested,* per se, but can still serve you extremely well in the business world and lead you toward a highly successful career. There are some soft skills that are taught in schools, such as critical thinking or media analysis. But regardless of where you acquired your soft skills, they can often be applied to a wider range of areas. That's the trade-off of hard and soft skills. Hard skills are easier to pin down and often are more directly employable, whereas soft skills are more transferable and tend to help you in a wider range of areas. Thus, you should make sure you have a solid combination of hard and soft skills in your repertoire to ensure that you will go far in your business.

How to Find Out Your Strengths and Weaknesses

So, how do you know what skills you do have? How can you really pin down the things you are good at so that you can start building your business around them? Well, in this section, we will look at some great strategies for you to figure out what your strengths are.

Strategy #1: Reflect on Your Feedback

One of the best ways is by thinking about how other people have received you and your talents. What kinds of things have you gotten praise for in the past? Have people always complimented your baking? Did you win awards for conflict resolution and empathy in school? Do you always seem to just get math problems faster than other people? Or, on the other hand, have you

TEEN ENTREPRENAIRE | 67

always just had a hard time speaking up in class? Do you just never seem to crack the "hidden meaning" of a book like everyone else can? Do you get winded running only a few strides? These might be examples of weaknesses, but you should really try to not beat yourself up about them. As we will see in the next section, weaknesses don't have to spell failure for your business. They can also be opportunities for you to admit your shortcomings and play to different strengths. Reflecting on the kinds of feedback that you have gotten throughout your life can be a great way to really discover what you are good at.

Strategy #2: Try Things Out

Since you're still young, there's likely a lot of things that you haven't even tried yet in your life. You might not have traveled on your own, been in a serious relationship, or tried playing a musical instrument. You really have no idea yet what you might or might not be good at. That's why, at this stage of life, it's always best to try things out before you judge yourself as bad at them. So, before you jump into your business journey assuming what you might or might not be good at, try some things first. Who knows? You might discover a talent you didn't even know you had!

Strategy #3: Make Lists

Sometimes, writing things down can really help you visualize them much better than having them simply floating around in your head. For this reason, it can be a great idea to just grab a pen and start jotting down things that you're good at. Nothing is off limits. You can go big or small, from knowing how to use photoshop to always being able to guess people's ages accurately. Whatever your skills are, make sure to list them. This is true for weaknesses as well, list all the things you're insecure about. You might find that, once they're down on the page, they don't seem so bad after all. This exercise can be really good for grounding you and making sure you know all the things you might be good at—or not so good at.

How to Play to Strengths

So, now that you know your strengths and weaknesses, you need to know how to actually use this knowledge to your advantage. Luckily, there are a lot of great ways. Here, we will look at some excellent strategies for capitalizing on your strengths.

Strategy #1: Put Hard Skills First

Because hard skills are usually more discipline-specific than soft skills, it's important to put them first when you are creating your business. Look for the areas where you have hard skills and try to steer your business in that direction. So, say you have a lot of arts-and-crafts skills, you could try making a business around selling hand-made items. Or say you are amazing at comprehending math skills; you could start a small business around after-school tutoring. These kinds of aims can help you really zero in on your hard skills and make sure that you are working with your strengths, not against them.

Strategy #2: Don't Underestimate Soft Skills

At the same time, it's important to make sure that you play to your soft skills as well, but they should come secondary. Instead of dictating what your business should be, they should dictate how it should be run. So, let's take the above two examples. Say you're really good at arts and crafts, but you're also a really big people person. Instead of selling online, you might want to try to sell at local art venues or farmer's markets so that your personality can shine through your in-person experience. As you can see, combining your hard skills and soft skills will help you to get the best possible experience for you and your customers.

Strategy #3: Work in Minor Skills

Remember those really minor skills we talked about above? Well, you can always try to incorporate those into your business idea as well. It's always best to try to pack in as many of these kinds of skills as possible, helping you to really showcase all of your strengths and make your business the absolute best it can be. If you have very small skills, such as making playlists or dressing yourself with the right colors, you should try to play these up as much as possible. For example, maybe you could curate an amazing lineup of music for your arts market to attract more customers or offer an extra service to match your scarf colors to your customer's ideal flattering shade. These skills might seem small, but as we can see from the above examples, they can really go a long way. Using these smaller skills can really take your business from great to exceptional and give it a unique twist.

How to Overcome Weaknesses

Now, you might also be wondering: What do I do about my weaknesses? How can I overcome those areas where I just don't naturally excel? Well, you have nothing to worry about. There are plenty of ways that you can completely obliterate the obstacles that your weaknesses might be causing you. In this section, we will look at some of the best strategies for overcoming your weaknesses.

Strategy #1: Sidestepping

The easiest way to avoid the pitfalls of your weaknesses in your business is to simply avoid them. Find work-arounds so that you won't have to encounter them. Bonus points if you are able to make this work-around part of your brand. For example, if you really struggle with web design, try making your knitting company the "offline" company, with a really bare-bones website and a more in-person feel. This way, you can appeal to people's nostalgia and online fatigue while also avoiding the skill that you really struggle with. It's all about making your weaknesses work for you!

Strategy #2: Outsourcing

If you have something that is absolutely necessary for your company; but you just don't feel confident enough about it, then you could try simply outsourcing it. This could be to an employee, freelancer, or even automation if that's possible. Let's take the example of web design again. You have a few options for that. On one hand, you could take on a business partner who does have that skill, thus, gaining it for your business. You could also go on Upwork and hire someone to design your website for you. Or, as a third option, you could use an easy website maker like Wordpress or Squarespace to help you through the process on a more automated level. These options will help you gain access to the skills you need without revealing your weakness.

Strategy #3: Upskilling

Every shortcoming is just an opportunity for growth, right? Instead of assuming that you will never be good at the thing you are struggling with, you could instead adopt a growth mindset and actually try to get better at it. Look at this shortcoming as an opportunity to upskill and maybe gain some new insights that will help with your business. Instead of avoiding creating a website or hiring someone else to do it, you could learn. Consider taking a course, even a cheap, online one, to help you demystify some of the process. You might find that the challenges you were particularly hung up on are actually fairly minimal once you have them explained to you. Once you are finished with this option, you will have gained a skill for life and won't ever need to outsource or sidestep this weakness again!

4

FIND YOUR NICHE

> "There's no path to success. Everyone constructs their own path. The important thing is to follow your heart. Find your niche, is my best advice."
>
> — KAROL G.

Once you have discovered all that makes you tick, you need to start putting your business plan into action. There are two main components to the starting of a business: the idea and the plan. The idea is all about what the business actually is: the model and the customer base. The plan is how you are going to execute that idea, looking more at growth and logistics. Both of these things are instrumental to making sure that your business starts out on the right foot.

In this chapter, we will go through the method of starting a business from this perspective. First, we will discuss the importance of your business idea itself. We'll talk about how the initial idea for your business contributes to your overall success and also give you some ideas about what kind of business you might want to start. Then, we will talk about how to choose the right business, giving you some pointers on which business might be best suited to your needs. After that, we will talk about some inspirational success stories that can get your ideas flowing for how you want to start your own business. And finally, we will talk about goal setting, which is one of the most instrumental skills involved in business and will help you start turning your business idea into a reality. Throughout the chapter, you should begin to get a strong sense of your own identity as a businessperson and start to build the foundation of your business idea.

THE IMPORTANCE OF THE IDEA

Every great business starts with an idea. Of course, the rest of the work, such as marketing, development, and good, old-fashioned elbow grease, are all important. But it is the initial idea that, if it is good, will lay the foundation for your entire business. You can think of your initial business ideas as being kind of like the foundation of a building. If you build a house on a foundation that is shoddily made, then it doesn't matter how well-built the house is, it will always be wobbly. Of course, you can also build a shoddy house on a strong foundation, but we will get to that later. The important thing is that your idea isn't just something that pops into your head and then you go out and make it a reality.

Ideas require refinement, consideration. You have to make sure that what you are envisioning for your business is feasible, unique, and has growth potential. Going through these refinements will help turn your idea from a faint inspiration into that strong, air-tight idea that your business needs to rest on. So, in this section, we will discuss some of the best questions to ask yourself to refine your business idea into the best it can be.

Question #1: What Problem Does it Solve?

Every great business finds a way to fill the gaps in people's lives. Maybe, it's access to foods that suit their dietary preferences. Maybe, it's a delivery service that is faster and more customized than ever before. Or maybe it's a tutoring service that accommodates online learning. Whatever the gap is, you need to find it because it will be the key to marketing your business going forward. Think about your business idea and ask yourself this question: How does this make the world a better place? How does this help people access something they couldn't access before? Asking yourself these questions can help you truly understand what makes your business unique and sets it apart from all the other small businesses out there.

Question #2: Who Is it For?

The next step toward refining your idea is to think about your target audience. What kind of person do you want to reach? What is their age range? What income bracket do they fit into? What are their interests, goals, fears, fantasies, etc.? Before you start your business, you really need to begin by drawing up your vision of this prospective customer. This will help you, particularly during the marketing stage when you will be figuring out who to target and how.

You can also incorporate market research into this stage. Think about your prospective customer base, and then go out and interview some of them. You can even ask them about your specific business idea and get their feedback on whether it would be something they're interested in. These interviews can be incredibly helpful because they can give you real-world insights into how the average consumer might react to your type of product. Make sure to take this feedback seriously. Obviously, you shouldn't get too discouraged by negative feedback, not to the point where you give up, but if a customer points out a flaw in your business plan, you might want to listen to them. Chances are, if they are picking up on this flaw, then other customers will too, so you should make sure that you do something to address it. This stage can really help your business change and grow as you start to let it interact with the rest of the world.

Question #3: How Does it Differ From Existing Businesses?

This is where you really start to think about what is unique about your business. It's all very well to have a great idea, but if someone is already out there doing it, then you're going to have a hard time convincing people to try your product instead of theirs. There always room at the table for lots of people to create similar small businesses, but if you want to be truly great, you are going to have to market your idea as somehow better or more special than others.

Again, this is a great time to try some market research. Go online, or to the mall (depending on your business type) and check out other businesses that offer a similar product or service to yours. This can be really helpful for a few reasons. For one, it can give you inspiration for things like marketing and even new products to add to your menu. But on the other hand, it can also help you scope out the competition and make sure to differentiate yourself from what they're doing.

For example, say you go to the arts market and see that another stall is selling hand-knitted scarves. However, their gimmick is that they will knit people's names into the fabric. If that was your plan, it's probably best not to do the same thing. Consider a different gimmick, like making custom patterns or matching sets. You could even market yourself as the sustainability brand, using completely sustainably sourced wool, or the fashion brand, taking inspiration from the Milan runway. Understanding what others are doing will help you to start carving out a unique niche for yourself.

BEST BUSINESS IDEAS FOR TEENS

So, you're aware of how important the initial idea is for your business. All you have to do is come up with that and you will have a stellar project. However, this is easier said than done. Coming up with a high-quality idea that is unique can actually be fairly difficult. You might not have the right inspiration, or the right know-how to actually come up with a feasible business idea. So, we are here to help! Here are some of the best business ideas for teens who are just starting out on their own.

Idea #1: Tutoring

If you are a person who has always succeeded academically, why not start a tutoring business? You can tutor kids a few grades below you so that you are more intimately familiar with the subject matter. You can even tutor online and set your scope to the global scale, tutoring kids in other countries. This can be a great business idea that has the potential to take you far in the world.

Idea #2: House and Pet Sitting

If you live in a residential area, chances are you have a lot of neighbors that have pets or plants that need care. With this in mind, you can make a great living promising to water people's plants or feed their pets while they're away. The best part of this idea is that you can often do more than one at the same time, since the job only takes a few minutes. Schedule a few clients within walking distance of one another and you're golden!

Idea #3: Outdoor Landscaping

Many people hate doing their outside chores. If you're handy, you like to be outdoors, or you have a bit of a green thumb, you could offer to do outside chores for people. You might end up watering or mowing lawns, raking leaves, or even doing some light gardening. If you live in a snowier region, you can even transition to snow-removal tasks in the winter. This business is great because it allows you to have a variety of regular gigs, and thus, a more regular income.

Idea #4: Handmade Crafts

If you're creative, you could consider selling your crafts. You could do it at school, door-to-door, or even at an arts market stall. One of the best ways to get a lot of customers is to work on commission. This basically means that you make custom crafts at your patron's request, maybe even with some personal details woven in so that they can have something truly unique. If you build a name for yourself, this could be a really lucrative business to get into.

Idea #5: Blogger or Podcaster

Do you have something to say to the world? Maye it's a niche interest that you could talk about for hours? Well, you could consider getting into blogging or podcasting. You might not see revenue right away from this type of business, but you will certainly be able to build a brand and name for yourself. You could even pair your blog with something that you are selling, such as your art, helping to tie them into one another. Either way, sharing your thoughts with the world through blogging and podcasting can be a great business idea as well as an awesome way to express yourself.

Idea #6: Photographer

If you've always been good with cameras, consider putting yourself out there as a freelance photographer. People are always looking for professional photoshoots to help them set up a resume, collect headshots for acting auditions, or even announce engagements or graduations. Network at school and with family friends to try to find events to photograph. This can be a super fun and creative business to sink your teeth into.

HOW TO CHOOSE THE RIGHT BUSINESS FOR YOU

Between the businesses listed above, and the many more that you might be able to think of, there are a lot of different businesses to choose from. Finding out which one is right for you can actually be a bit of a daunting task. We've already discussed at length how to figure out what your interests are and where your strengths lie, but what about the other factors? What about the more logistical or practical concerns that might come into play when deciding what field you want to go into or what kind of business you want to run? Here, we will discuss some of the more logistical concerns about your business decisions, listing some important factors that you might want to consider before starting your own business.

Factor #1: Time

Running a business takes a lot of time out of your day. Therefore, you have to figure out how your business fits into your existing schedule. Factors might include whether you study at an in-person school or you are homeschooled, whether you do any after school activities, and what your social life looks like. If you are someone who doesn't have a lot of free time, then you might want to choose a business with fewer regular commitments. That way, if you get busier, during exam season, for instance, then you will be able to take a break. You should also think about other constraints you might have in your life. For example, if you want to have a lawn mowing business, but your family tends to go up to the cottage for the summer, that might not be a feasible option for you. Instead, you could choose a business like knitting scarves, that you can do from anywhere, creating a backlog of inventory that you can sell when you get back. Examining the time and logistical constraints of your life will help you to consider what kind of business will work with your schedule and lifestyle.

Factor #2: Profitability

As we discussed in the list of potential businesses, some are going to be more profitable, and some may offer more instant returns than others. Every business has a growth period where you have to get the word out, but there will be some that allow you to profit sooner or in larger amounts than others. For example, a business where you provide a service will usually result in you profiting sooner than a business where you are selling products. This is because you have to account for the amount of time it takes to make the items and any money you have to spend on materials. Whereas things like pet care or house sitting don't require any preparation or materials. If you are looking to get into something that is profitable quickly, then you should try to find something that doesn't require much preparation time and doesn't have much overhead.

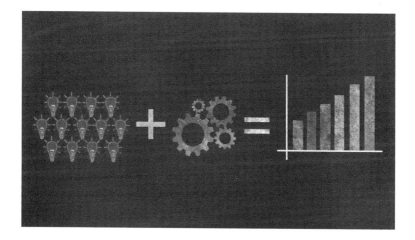

Factor #3: Growth Potential

The other factor you might want to think about is your potential for growth. If your business is something you could continue to expand, then it has growth potential. You will eventually reach a point where you have more work than you have time to handle it all. This is when you can start hiring people and expanding outward. Your employees will benefit from your skills in building and networking with clients, and you will be able to expand your business without having to do all the work yourself. If this is something that you are interested in, then you should seek out a business that has high growth potential. Luckily, with online resources at your disposal, you can now expand infinitely on a global level. Shipping your products around the world can help you to expand your business beyond your local area.

SETTING GOALS

Once you have decided on your business and its style, you need to figure out what your goals are. What are you trying to accomplish with your business? How do you see it playing out, and at what pace? These will be your goals for the actual execution of your business. You can generally break these down into short- and long-term goals. On the short-term side, you have the immediate things that you want to accomplish with your business. These are the smaller achievements, the ones that you will be able to obtain in the near future. The long-term goals are the things you want to see happen with your business over time, the future places you want it to go. These can really be shoot-for-the-stars dreams, the kinds of goals that you might not be able to directly imagine yourself achieving, but that excite you, nonetheless. In this section, we will talk about some of the most important short- and long-term goals you should be thinking about for your business.

Short-Term Goals

Over the first six months to a year of your company, you should be trying to accomplish short-term goals. This first period might have a lot of bumps in the road and times when it seems like your business just isn't succeeding. But if you keep your eyes on your goals, you should be able to push through. These goals are smaller, but they are still extremely important foundations for your business's future. Making sure you accomplish these goals—and accomplish them well—is integral to establishing your business. In this section, we will give you three essential short-term goals to work toward in the first year or so of your business.

Making a Profit

The first thing you want to do when you are starting a business is to actually make a profit. This might not sound like a novel concept, but it can take a little while to accomplish. You shouldn't feel too badly about yourself if you aren't profiting in the first few months. You have to spend money to make money, and many businesses require a large initial investment before they actually start turning a profit. However, you should still set your sights on making a profit some time in that year. Look to the next two goals to see how you can grow your business enough in that time to see those first profits materialize.

Establishing a Brand

The next important thing you want to do is establish your brand. What is your gimmick or unique quality as a company? It can be as flashy as offering special, personalized experiences, or as simple as providing quality, hand-done work. You can also include other things in your brand, such as community outreach (i.e., donating a certain percentage of your profits to a charity) or sustainability (i.e., committing to a zero-carbon production process) in order to show your business's humanitarian side. You can also create some branded materials, perhaps with an eye-catching logo or a signature color to help customers remember you in the future. These qualities can work to set you apart from other companies and help you to really start establishing your business.

Building a Customer Base

And finally, you want to build a solid base of customers. There are generally two types of businesses: repeat customer businesses and one-time purchase businesses. A repeat customer business would be anything where your average customer is going to keep coming back with an ever-renewing need for your products or services. Examples would be lawn care, tutoring, or selling any edible product. In the early days of this kind of business, customer retention is crucial. You want to develop a strong relationship with those first few customers so that you can guarantee that they keep coming back consistently. If you have this kind of business, you should really emphasize customer relations and maintaining those connections through personalization and showing your unique personality.

The second type of business—one-time purchases—has a different model, one where your product or service is generally something the average customer will only buy once or twice. This could be any business where you sell a product that is not perishable or a service that is required less frequently. Examples could be wool sweaters or house painting. In either of these cases, people will likely only seek out your services a few times. After all, you only need your rooms painted a finite number of times and can only own so many custom wool sweaters. However, customer relations are still highly important at this stage, since you can get a lot of work through word of mouth. So, for example, your house painting customer might not need you to paint any more rooms, but they could potentially recommend you to a friend, who then recommends you to a friend, creating a lucrative network of customers. For this reason, you should still prioritize customer relations in this line of work.

That being said, in one-time-purchase type businesses, you should focus more heavily on advertising. In repeat customer work, a few good clients can keep you going for a long time. But in the one-time-purchase line of work, it's all about the next customer. In this case, you should invest a greater percentage of your overhead into advertising. This could be posters you hang around the community, sponsored posts on social media, or even a radio or newspaper spot if you have an older demographic. Because a constant flow of customers is essential in one-time-purchase work, you should make sure that you are consistently advertising and getting as many customers as you possibly can.

Long-Term Goals

Once you have achieved your short-term goals and created a successful business in its early stages, you want to start working toward your long-term goals. This is not to say that you shouldn't always have these long-term goals in the back of your mind from day one. On the contrary—you should absolutely always be thinking about your long-term goals. They will be the guiding force of your business's ethos throughout your entire journey. However, accomplishing your short-term goals will help you to shift your focus toward the long-term goals for your business. In this section, we will give you three different long-term goals that you should be working into your future business plans.

Making a Difference

In the section about doing what you love, we talked a little about how important it is to make a difference with your business. Regardless of whether you want to donate to charitable institutions, you should think about what your business is doing for the world. Even just offering people access to something they did not have access to previously can be a way of making a difference in the world. Maybe being a living-wage employer, making sure all your employees are making a fair wage, is your way of making a difference. Whatever it is, you will feel much better about yourself, and your business will have a stronger focus if you commit to making a difference in the world in some way.

Innovating in Your Field

Another great long-term goal to have as an entrepreneur is to innovate in some way. If you have already made sure that your company has a unique quality that will help you stand out, then congratulations! You have already done a significant part of this. If you are doing something that no one has done before, then you are already innovating in that field. This long-term goal will not only help you create a much better company that will be more lucrative for your future, but also, it will secure your legacy. If you want to be remembered as a truly great entrepreneur, it's essential that you do something innovative. So, make sure that you are really making something solid and use your business as an opportunity to create something groundbreaking.

Financial Freedom

Finally, one of the main reasons that people want to be an entrepreneur is to achieve financial freedom. Financial freedom is essentially the opportunity to have passive income and thus not have to work for your money. You will be able to travel, pursue other interests, and enjoy the finer things in life, all while running a successful business. This is a dream for many entrepreneurs, and it is perfectly achievable for you if you want it.

IT CAN FEEL LIKE YOU HAVE A
MILLION LESSONS TO LEARN RIGHT
NOW. IT'S ONLY NATURAL TO NEED
HELP FILTERING THE CRUCIAL
ONES!

"You will either learn to manage money, or the lack of it will manage you."

— DAVE RAMSEY

You, like many other teens, have probably sat through dozens of classes and lectures wondering if that information is going to be necessary for your future. Unless your career is aimed at such areas, do you really need to recite the periodic table or identify metaphors in poetry?

Most teenagers spend these classes imagining the future, becoming financially free, and living life to the max. They conjure up an image of the house they will live in and the car they will drive. Maybe even early retirement to travel the world.

Just as the sound of the bell wakes you out of the dream — reality hits. Your parents probably had all the same dreams but unfortunately, they are slugging away at their careers, stressed out, and barely making ends meet.

Whether you have $5 in your pocket in $100, now is the time to start managing your finances. And you have taken some of the fundamental steps in doing so. The financial skills you have learned so far and going to set you up for effective money management and doing something that you love.

You will be able to take all of your creativity and new-found time-management skills to lay the foundations for success. But why stop there?

Robert Nay was 14 and with no coding experience when he created the game app Bubble Ball. In 2 weeks his game had been downloaded more than a million times, overtaking the then-popular Angry Birds. He earned $2 million in just 2 weeks! Now 17, he uses his talent to create games to help children learn spelling and reading.

You too can be a teen entrepreneur and help others!

By sharing your views on this book, other teens who are worried about their financial future can discover what needs to be done to see a positive change in their lives.

It just takes a few minutes and I will be extremely grateful if you could give others a helping hand too.

5

GETTING STARTED

> *"Opportunity does not waste time with those who are unprepared."*
>
> — IDOWU KOYENIKAN

So, you've thought of the idea for your business, you've laid the groundwork, set your goals, and decided what you want your mission to be. Where do you go from here? Well, now you actually have to start getting your business off the ground. You have to learn how to start your business and put it in motion. This might seem like an intimidating stage, but it really doesn't have to be. With the right know-how and gumption, you can make the process of actually starting your business very smooth. In this chapter, we are going to walk you through the most important steps on the path to starting your business.

First, we will give you a comprehensive checklist of the basic materials and permits you are going to need before you start your business. Then, we will look at all the distinct steps to planning your business. After that, we will talk about finding the materials and the space you'll need to conduct your business's operations. Following this, we will talk about some of the best strategies for finding customers. And finally, we will talk about a less interesting but infinitely important step in starting a business: filing your taxes. By the end of the chapter, you should be very confident about the steps that will be required to start a business and some of the more logistical parts of the process will be demystified.

WHAT YOU NEED BEFORE YOU START A BUSINESS

Before you start a business, there are actually some important legal requirements you need to clear. Every kind of business is different and so you will have to research the specific type of business that you want to start, but generally, these are the most important legal requirements that you will need to fulfill in order to start a successful business.

Requirement #1: Trademarking and Copyright

If you look in the corner of any major brand name or logo, you will usually find a little ©, ™, or ® sign. These are copyright signs, indicating that the company has a trademark. Trademarks are essentially designed to make sure no one steals another business's work. With this safeguard, they can continue to sell their product or service without worrying about being ripped off. You should be concerned about trademarks and copyright for two reasons. The first reason is that you absolutely do not want to violate anyone else's copyright. If you start to get successful, you might attract their attention and risk getting sued. This is not what you want. Thus, you should make sure you do a lot of research before you try to start a business. Make sure your business model, your logo, your name, and any other things associated with your business are unique. You don't want your work to closely resemble anyone else's work. You'll thank yourself in the long run when you avoid getting sued.

The second reason why you should be concerned about trademarking is that you might want to do it yourself. In the early days of your business, this probably isn't necessary. You aren't going to have the resources to sue anyone, and you won't have a large enough customer base for others to steal anyway. So, before you start your business, especially as a teen, you don't need to worry about trademarks or copyright. Save this for down the road. On the other hand, if you have a logo or a device that is particularly distinctive, and you have enough funds initially to pay for a patent, you can absolutely go for it! Just make sure that it's worth your money.

Requirement #2: Permits

Depending on the kind of business you are trying to run, you may need to get permits. The things that require permits usually involve food service, working with children, or working with animals. If you are selling crafts that you make at home, then you probably don't need a license, but if you open a stall where you sell your homemade baked goods, then you will have to get permits and follow all your local area's health and safety codes for food service. So, if the business you're building is in one of these more vulnerable sectors (involving food, children, or pets), then it's up to you to make sure you have all the required permits and licenses.

Requirement #3: Employment Laws

If you are going to be hiring anyone else for your business, either to help you make your website or to share some of the workload with you, then you absolutely need to make sure that you are complying with all of the labor laws for your area. You need to make sure that you don't violate any labor laws, and that you are paying an hourly rate that is at least the legal minimum. These laws and the minimum wage will vary depending on where you live, so make sure you do all the proper research before you start your business to avoid breaking any of these very important rules.

Requirement #4: Music Licensing Laws

This one is often overlooked, but it's actually very important. There are strict rules about when you can play music inside your business and when you can't. So, if you are going to be setting up a stall or a shop, you need to make sure you have the rights to the music that you are playing. You can't just pop on your Spotify account and let your favorite songs play. Even though it might seem harmless, it is actually a copyright violation. Playing the radio is also considered to be in violation of these rules. You can acquire a music license from a place like PPL and that will allow you to play music in your business, so if that is something you really want to do, then you can look into that as an option.

PLANNING YOUR BUSINESS

You've already set some goals and decided on the premise for your business, but this is different from actually planning it. When it comes down to your business plan, you have to get into the specifics. This plan is going to be the basis on which you hang your whole business. It should include everything from the amount of money you are going to spend on everything to your company's name and where you are going to conduct your business. Here, we are going to list the major steps you should be taking when starting to plan your business.

Step 1: Name and Logo

Before you can actually start making your products, you have to come up with a name. There are two main types of company names: the ones that are really sleek and innovative, and the ones that are simple. The simple kind can be something like: "The [your name] [type of business] Company." An example of this would be Kylie Cosmetics, by Kylie Jenner. You can also try the format: "[your city] [type of company]". A good example of this would be LA Fitness. Both of these tell you exactly what they are, and either who made them or where they are located. These simpler names have an advantage. The biggest advantage to this kind of name is that you will likely show up much more easily on search engines. Anyone looking for that service in your city will be able to easily find you, and they will know who you are and what you do right away.

The second type of name is sleeker, sometimes named after a symbol, and usually doesn't have to do with the purpose of the company itself—think Apple, Bumble, or Firefox. These names are more ambiguous, but they can help customers to remember you more easily. Plus, you can always make up for your searchability by including a lot of important keywords on your website. You can also opt for the hybrid option, where you create a name that is a composite of the type of company you want to start and a cool image or pun. Pizza Nova or Planet Fitness are both great examples of this. So, when naming your company, make sure to take into account the different kinds of names that you could possibly use.

In addition to names, you also want to create a logo. Now, you don't always have to hire a graphic designer to come up with a clever symbol for your business. A logo can be as simple as an iconic font. Think about Harry Potter or Star Wars. Those fonts are so recognizable that they don't even need a logo attached for people to make the association. Coming up with a distinctive (but still easy to read) font to write your business name can be a great way to help you stick out in a subtler way.

If you want to design a logo, you need to think about the different types. There are abstract logos that might be just generic symbols—think the Nike swoosh—or there are literal logos, which usually directly relate either to the business at hand—such as Burger King— or with the symbol attached to the company—such as Target. Look to all these logos for inspiration and see which kind feels like it best suits you and your company.

Step 2: Creating a Budget

After you've created the name and the look for your company, you need to start thinking about how much everything is going to cost. There are two main components to your costs as a business. First of all, you have your startup costs. These are the initial costs that you will have to pay right away when you start your business. They might be licensing fees, buying your first batch of materials, a down payment or deposit on a space, and even other expenses like hiring people to design your website or logo. These initial costs might seem like a lot, but they are very worthwhile investments if they lead to you being able to start your successful business.

The other type of costs is ongoing. These are costs that you will continually have to account for as you continue to operate your business. These expenses can be anything from rent on your space and cost of materials to the salaries of your employees. These expenses need to be very closely budgeted against any of your projected earnings. As your company grows, your expenses will likely grow as well. However, if you have made sure to always keep your earnings above your expenses, then you will be able to grow at a steady rate without overextending yourself. To make your budget, write out every single expense you can possibly foresee. Work out exactly how much you will need for your startup costs and how much you will need to make every month to cover your ongoing costs.

Step 3: The How, What, and Where

The next major step in your company is figuring out the how, what, and where of your business. The how is the actual way you are going to provide your product or service. Are you going to be selling online, conducting in-person classes, borrowing your parents' car? This initial "how" is basically the structure of your business. It is the logistical setup. In this stage of figuring out your business, you need to know about things like your transportation, your relationship with your customers, and what kind of service you are going to be providing. You should also have a good idea of how long each service will take (i.e., 30-minute tutoring sessions) or how long it takes you to make each product (i.e., five hours to knit a sweater). Knowing these "how" factors will bring you much closer to all the logistical concerns of your company.

The "what" factor is all about your materials. These are the things you need to run your business. They can be the materials needed to create your products (i.e., wool for sweaters, baking ingredients for cookies, etc.) but also any secondary materials you might need to facilitate the running of your business (i.e., piano books for lessons, a vehicle to access remote locations, etc.). These primary and secondary materials will be very important to your startup budget, so make sure you really account for them and don't leave anything out. You have to know what kind of materials you want to use (i.e., organic, hand-dyed wool vs. synthetic wool), how much these materials cost, and where you are going to source them from (i.e., wholesalers vs. craft stores).

And finally, you should have the "where" ironed out. This will be where you operate your service, where you make your products, and where you sell them. Include places where you think your prospective customers are going to live, especially if your service involves going to their houses. So, say you are running a lawn-mowing company, you will have to limit the distance you are willing to go for your business. You'll want to schedule clients that are within walking distance, public transport distance, or within a 15-minute drive if you have access to a vehicle. Remember: You don't get paid for transportation, so set travel limits early on. (Make sure to include any transportation costs, such as gas money or a bus pass, into your monthly budget.)

If you are going to be hosting people for your services, make sure you have a clean, professional-looking space in your house and that you have cleared it with the rest of your family members. If you are going to be making products, you should also make sure you have a dedicated workspace where you can make them without having to clean up every few hours (i.e., not the kitchen table or your bed—try to have a space just for your craft). And finally, you should also know where you are going to sell your products. Do research into setting up an online store, or a stall at a local arts market to start establishing your business. Having all these logistics figured out will bring you one step closer to starting your business for real.

Step 4: Finding Investors

Remember when we talked about those initial startup costs you need to consider when you are creating your own business? Well, they are sometimes hard to come by, especially for a teen who might not have a lot of their own money. Fortunately, there is something called an investor. An investor is a person who gives you money to start your business under the condition that they receive a percentage of the profits later on. So, they might give you $1,000 to buy supplies, but then ask that you give them 10% of all your profits going forward. Sometimes, they will even ask for a share in your company, meaning that they have a 10% say in how the company is run, in addition to 10% of the profits. These numbers are just an example and will completely depend on how the investor evaluates your company.

Generally, they will buy shares in your company based on how much potential they think you have. The idea is that they will make back their money and then some, assuming your company continues to grow. Having an investor early on is a great win-win. You get the initial money to start your business and they get to see a return on their money down the road. To really under-stand how investing works and to see some of the best ways to pitch to an investor, you can watch shows like Shark Tank (or Dragon's Den in the UK and Canada), but here are some general pointers on how to get and pitch to an investor.

Tip #1: Evaluate Your Company Fairly

One of the biggest mistakes you will see people make on shows like Shark Tank is evaluating their company way too highly. People with just an idea might ask for $100,000 dollars for only 1% of their company, which is actually an evaluation of $10,000,000! To pitch fairly to investors and make sure you are offering them a fair deal, do a simple calculation to figure out your compa-ny's value. Generally, the value of a company is calcu-lated by taking your assets (everything you own, including already-made stock) and subtracting your liabilities (any expenses). So, say you own $1000 in equipment and stock, and you have $100 in liabilities, your company would be valued at $900. So, you could ask investors to contribute $90 for 10% of your company and that would be a fair price.

Tip #2: Have Some Proven Success First

Even though your investors are likely partially investing in you and your personality, they also like to see that you have some proven success. If you are able to make any sales or score any customers before you get an investor, then you will be able to show them that your business is viable and has potential for growth. This will also allow you to make profit projections, which investors love to see. So, say you make $500 in your first month. That probably means you are going to make at least $6,000 over the course of the year, and potentially more if you are able to get investors and score more clients. Being able to make such a projection—and having the sales numbers to back it up—will make investors more comfortable investing their money in you, since you have shown you are capable of making their money back for them. It's all about maintaining that strong relationship.

Tip #3: Don't Give Away Too Much Too Fast

It might be tempting to see a huge lump sum of spending money at the beginning of your business, but this usually comes with a hefty percentage of profits that you have to sign away. If an investor is offering you a lot of money, but they are going to take 30, 40, or even worse, 50% of your company, you should look very closely at that deal and examine whether you absolutely need that money. The more of your company you give away at the beginning, the less control you will have over it and the fewer profits you will have down the road. This is especially true for anything over 50%, since the investor will have a higher stake in your company than you do, which can get very bad. Investors are great in small doses, so don't let lots of money fool you into giving too much away too fast—chances are, you're going to make way more than that in the long run, so hold out.

Tip #4: Consider an Investor Mentor

That being said, investors are also great as mentors. They will usually be adults and many of them are experienced entrepreneurs, themselves. If you find someone who is really passionate about you and your business, that can be one of the best experiences you can get as an entrepreneur. Being able to pick that person's brain and benefit from their advice can be truly priceless to a young entrepreneur like yourself. Therefore, choose your investors wisely and make sure you are only working with people who truly believe in your vision and want to help you.

Step 5: Finding Customers

The final major step to setting up your business is finding your customer base. This is one of the most important—and also the hardest—parts of starting a business. You essentially have to sell yourself to each customer that comes your way. However, customers can also be like a good kick off on a bike. If you get a few going at the beginning, you can gain momentum and start to add more customers exponentially. Word of mouth, good reviews on your website or social media, and even just lessons learned can help your small customer base balloon really quickly. But finding those first few customers can be tricky. Here are some great tips for how to get the ball rolling with your businesses.

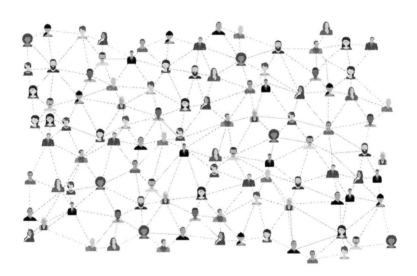

Tip #1: Advertise

The most obvious thing you should do to initially attract customers is to advertise. You can advertise in many different ways, especially nowadays with so many reasonably priced (or even free) online advertising options. You can go the old-fashioned route, putting up posters around the neighborhood. Or, you can make a post on Facebook or Instagram and ask friends and family to share it, or even boost it as a sponsored post. You can ask your friends and family to spread the word by mouth to try to get a chain reaction going. However you can get your name and business out there, do it! Although, one important thing to keep in mind is demographics.

Think about the ages and life situations of those you are marketing to. If you are looking to mow lawns, you should be advertising to homeowners and those who are adults to middle aged, and so posters and leaflets might work well. But if you are looking to sell your trendy jewelry to other teens, you could try advertising at school or on your social media accounts. Bear in mind your business's style and the kind of customer you are trying to attract before you advertise.

Tip #2: Offer Special Deals

Another way to get people in the door quickly is to offer discounted prices for the first few customers. You can even offer your services for free if you want! This can either be an effort to gain a good reputation for yourself, build skills, or even in explicit exchange for a review. For example, you could offer free lawn mowing to the first five customers, but they have to leave you a review. This way, you can establish some potentially regular customers, and start to build up some solid reviews on your profile or website. It's a win-win because people generally like getting free stuff and you will very easily boost your visibility in the community by quite a bit.

Tip #3: Partner With Another Business

One less common but still highly effective way of boosting your profile is to partner with an established business or even a charity. The way you do this is dependent on your type of business, but one thing you could do would be to hold a charity car wash while advertising your actual business. Or, you could ask a local thrift or arts-and-crafts store to carry your home-made soaps with your logo on them. Piggybacking off of another business or charity is not just a great way to boost your visibility, but also to make connections in your community!

FILING TAXES

And of course, the inevitable taxes. As inevitable as death, according to some people. If you are running a business, you are going to have to file taxes on it. This is a good thing! It allows your business to give back to the community as it takes from it. But the government also understands that not all the money you make from your business is actually profit. This is why they provide something called a "tax write-off."

When you file your taxes as a self-employed business owner, you can report all the money you spent on your business and have it taken off your taxable income.

This is because you technically had to spend that money in order to make your salary and thus it doesn't really count as income. So, let's say you made $5,000 in a year and are being taxed at 10%. That would mean you owe $500 in taxes. However, if you spent $1,000 in that year on your business, for expenses like materials and such, then you will actually only be taxed on $4,000 of your income. This means that you will only owe $400 in taxes, which is much better!

However, you can't just claim that you spent $1,000 on your business, you also have to prove it. Occasionally, the government will perform something called an "audit." An audit is essentially a spot check to make sure that people are filing their taxes properly. Anyone can be audited, from individuals to businesses to nonprofits. Generally, it is random, but businesses and nonprofits get audited more often. If you are going to have a business where you write off a lot of expenses, then you need to make sure you keep all your receipts and can justify every single penny you write off. So, don't try to get clever and write off things that you don't really need (like "work lunches" or trips that weren't 100% work-related). It's best to stay honest and not try to avoid the inevitability of taxes.

6

GROWING YOURSELF

"An investment in knowledge pays the best interest."

— BENJAMIN FRANKLIN

Pivoting away from the logistics of starting a business, let's talk a bit about you. Becoming an entrepreneur is, after all, about your personal journey as well. It is a learning experience where you will be finding out so many things about yourself and building so many incredible new skills. Thus, you have to make sure you are choosing the right paths in your entrepreneurial journey to make those leaps in yourself. In this chapter, we will highlight your personal journey as an entrepreneur, listing some of the most important lessons and skills that you should be gaining from this experience. We will list each of these important skills along with some tips on how to develop them, as well as some arguments for their importance. By the end of this chapter, you should have a firmer grasp on what it means to be an entrepreneur from the inside out.

FINANCE SKILLS

As we talked about way back in Chapter 1, you should have excellent financial skills before you start a business. But at that point in the book, we only really touched on the personal side of financial skills, or what you should be doing with your money once you've made it. There is a whole other side to financial skills that you need to understand before you start your company: the business side. If you can understand financial matters from a more businesslike perspective, then you will be able to fuse the financial skills you learned back in Chapter 1 with your business practices. Here are some of the most important financial skills you will need to know as an entrepreneur.

Skill #1: Business Budgeting

More than just budgeting for yourself, you also need to budget for your business. Much like personal budgeting, business budgeting is all about priorities. You need to find a way to really evaluate what your priorities are for your business if you want to have a proper budget. Some of the things you will need to budget for are materials, space expenses, travel expenses, advertising, and employees. The trick is figuring out what percentage of your business's expenses are going to go toward each of these things. This will completely depend on your type of company and how far along you are in growing your business. For example, in the early stages, you might want to budget a higher percentage for advertising to get your name out, then scale it back when you have a sizable customer base. Conversely, in the later stages of your business, you might want to devote a higher percentage of your income to hiring people, since it can really help you scale things up. As you can see, these different states of your business will have a massive effect on how you spend your money. You should take stock regularly so you know what you should be spending in any given area at any particular time.

Skill #2: Reinvesting Your Profits

Once you start making money from your business, you are going to be able to start paying yourself. Now, another key part of budgeting and making decisions about your business in general is whether to keep that money for yourself or reinvest it back into the business. Obviously, you want to be able to pay yourself for your efforts, but on the other hand, you also want to be able to grow your business. In this position, you should think of yourself as your own investor. Of course, you need to pay yourself, so figure out how much money you need to cover your own expenses, then think of the rest of the money as an investment in the future. Doing this will help you avoid having to get too many investors and will also help you scale your business at a rate you might not have thought was possible. So, when you make your first real profits, devote a considerable portion of them to the scaling of your business so that you can turn them into the future of your company.

Skill #3: Understanding the Value of Spending

Reading the last section, you were probably feeling a little discouraged. *You mean I can't enjoy my profits right away?* It might seem frustrating to have to wait until your profits really start to come in, but you will be able to see that it's worth it once you really understand the value of spending. Spending money is essential to any business. You have probably heard the expression "you have to spend money to make money," which is entirely true in this case. When you are running a business, you absolutely have to spend your money in order to generate profits. Spending money might sound bad, since most financial advice says to save as much as possible, but from a business standpoint, spending can actually be better than saving. It can allow you to grow your business, which means that your money is not getting *spent*, it is getting *invested*. So, don't shy away from spending when it is necessary.

TIME MANAGEMENT

Time. It's what we never feel like we have enough of. It can be really hard to manage your time as an entrepreneur, especially if you are also in school, do extracurricular activities, or have an active social life. As a teen entrepreneur, it's very easy to become overwhelmed by the amount of time you have to devote to your business on top of all your other obligations. If you don't learn how to manage your time effectively, you could be looking at a serious issue. In this section, we will give you some key tips for how you can manage your time a little better.

Tip #1: Know Your Value

One of the biggest mistakes that young entrepreneurs make is not knowing the value of their time. You might overwork yourself, make commitments you can't follow through on, or simply burn out. For this reason, you should be very careful to calculate how many hours you spend maintaining your business and how much money you are actually making per hour. Knowing your hourly rate and making a commitment to stick to it can help you keep your work in check. Make sure you know the value of your time before you get any deeper into being an entrepreneur.

Tip #2: Create a Time Budget

You know what they say: "Time is money!" If you're going to be creating elaborate budgets for your money, then why not do the same for your time? A huge mistake that you can make is to spend too much of your time on one thing, while neglecting another. For this reason, it's a great idea to create a time budget. Thus, you should figure out how much time per week or per day you will spend on your business in general, and how much of that time you should be spending on each task. So, say you can commit to spending 10 hours per week on your business. You then need to figure out how you should divide that time.

The majority will obviously be devoted to making your product or providing your service. But you also need to spend time networking, dealing with customer needs, advertising, and planning. These tasks take up more time than you would think, and so, just like the unexpected costs associated with your budget, you should make sure that you account for them. One "time budget" could look like spending 10% of your time dealing with customers, 5% of your time budgeting and planning, 5% of your time arranging advertising, and the remaining 80% on the product or service itself. This way, you will avoid spending too much time on one thing and will always be able to account for your time.

COMMUNICATION

If you pick up one entrepreneurial skill from reading this book, it should absolutely be communication. Whether you are communicating with the team of employees you have amassed, with your customers, or with the people you source materials from, being an entrepreneur is 90% communication. You need to be able to barter with people, hear their needs, and come across as a trustworthy, caring person. Again, you are not just selling your products, you are also selling *you*. In this section, we will talk about some of the key communication skills you should keep in your back pocket if you want to be an excellent entrepreneur.

Skill #1: Negotiation

In your time as an entrepreneur, you are very likely going to have to do a lot of negotiating. This might be for prices of materials or services, wages for employees, or even terms of your services to your customers. Negotiation is all about compromise and about maintaining a balance between your needs and the other person's needs. This requires you to have two simultaneous sub-skills: self-respect and consideration for others.

Self-respect is incredibly important when it comes to negotiation. If you lack self-respect, then you are simply going to let people walk all over you and will never be able to achieve what you want to. You will likely get bad deals and people will come to know you as someone who can be easily taken advantage of. At the same time, you also want to have equal respect for the other person. It might be tempting to low-ball everyone, but this can also backfire and cause people to feel disrespected. Instead, you should make it clear that you know you have a good product, but also that you don't think the other person it stupid. Thus, you make a fair deal, and everyone comes out feeling like they got what they wanted.

Skill #2: Self-Presentation

Part of communication is being conscious of how you come across to other people. As an entrepreneur, it's essential that you keep careful watch over your persona. One glaringly wrong move and you could completely undermine everything you have worked toward thus far. The first step toward achieving a good self-presentation is self-awareness. Be conscious of everything that you are: your look, your cadence of speech, how much you smile or say "um." All of these things are going to shape the way others perceive you, which can actually have a powerful effect on your future success as an entrepreneur. Try presenting a business pitch in front of the mirror or film yourself doing it. Do you notice anything about yourself that might be off-putting or weird? Coming across as a sociable person is a very important communication skill, so make sure you are always putting your best foot forward, especially when it comes to pitching and meeting new people.

LEADERSHIP

Being an entrepreneur is, after all, being a leader. You are not only going to be at the helm of your business, calling all the shots, but also, possibly, the leader of a team once you start hiring employees. Thus, you need to make sure you have exceptional leadership skills if you are going to be a successful entrepreneur. In this section, we will list some of the most important qualities in a leader so you can strive to embody them in your journey as an entrepreneur.

Quality #1: Integrity

No one wants to follow someone who doesn't believe in themself. To be a leader, you have to be true to who you are and wholeheartedly believe in what you are selling. This will lend authenticity to your brand and make sure that the people you are leading can really put their faith in you. But integrity isn't always easy. One of the most important components of integrity is the ability to admit that you're wrong. Being wrong isn't fun, but trying to cover it up or make it seem like you're not at fault can be much worse. Instead, make sure to practice accountability. You're new to this and there's no shame in making a few mistakes. Keeping honest and allowing yourself to learn—and even be vulnerable in front of employees—can actually end up earning you more respect. If you want to have integrity, you have to stay honest.

Quality #2: Vision

If you are leading people, you'd better know where you're going. Having a vision for the future is integral to being a successful leader. You have to make sure that the way forward looks possible and promising. For the people who are going to be following you, this future will be the thing that keeps them believing in you. Thus, not only do you have to have this promising vision—for the company or even for the world—in mind, but you also need to sell it well. People aren't going to understand your vision if you don't present it to them. Make sure you have clear goals for your company and a strong method of expressing them. This will help you to gain the trust of others and to lead your company toward success.

SELF-MOTIVATION AND MANAGEMENT

Part of being your own boss means that you actually have to motivate yourself. Bosses, managers, and supervisors are meant to motivate you and keep you on track. If you don't have them breathing down your neck, then you have to do that work all on your own. As nice as it is to not have to answer to a boss, it can also be difficult to regulate yourself to that degree. If you lack strong self-regulation, then you can risk getting lazy and procrastinating your work. This is why, as an entrepreneur, you have to learn to motivate yourself, to manage yourself, and to be your own boss the right way. Here are some excellent techniques for making sure that you stay on track, they can help you develop the important skill of self-regulation.

Technique #1: Setting Small Goals

You probably already know the overarching goals of your business, or even the short-term goals that you want to accomplish in the next few months. But even these short-term goals can be easy to procrastinate. If you don't have a strong focus for every single day that you are working on your business, then you will not be able to get things done at the rate you need to. This is why it can be immensely helpful to create small goals for yourself so that you can make sure every day comes with a sense of accomplishment. So, for example, one of your day's goals could be to print off your posters, then the next day could be to hang them around town. These small goals break up your larger goals, making them feel more manageable and helping you to stay on task.

Technique #2: Keep Reminders of Your Goals

When you're in the throes of working very hard at your business, it can be really tough to stay motivated. That's why having visual reminders of your goals, or even incentives, can be a great way to remind yourself what you're doing it all for. Say you want to eventually earn enough money to take a trip to Italy. Well, a great way to express this is to use a photo of the city you want to visit as your laptop or phone background to remind yourself of that ultimate goal. Or maybe you could write some inspirational quotes by your favorite CEOs and hang them on your wall to remind yourself of your heroes. These are small contributions, but they can actually make a huge difference in how much you will be able to motivate yourself.

7

BE PREPARED

> *"Being challenged in life is inevitable, being defeated is optional."*
>
> — ROGER CRAWFORD

Despite all the motivation in the world, there are going to be times in your entrepreneurial journey when things won't go your way. You are going to encounter setbacks, unfamiliar situations, and maybe even go through a period of loss. This is all normal to starting a business. There are inevitable twists and turns along the way that are all a common part of the process. However, it can be really easy to let these things get you down. Going through setbacks, especially early on in your business, can increase the risk of you quitting too early. Perseverance is, then, one of the biggest values you can have as a businessperson. That, and the ability to prepare both practically and mentally for these setbacks. In this chapter, we will lead you through some of the most common setbacks that entrepreneurs face in the early days of their businesses. After that, we'll let you in on some of the best ways to overcome them.

UNCLEAR BUSINESS PLANS

More than other people or events that can set you back in life, you can actually set yourself back. The first thing you should really be watching out for when it comes to early setbacks is not having a clear enough business plan. This can be a lack of air-tight budgeting, a huge logistical gap that you haven't filled, or even unrealistic expectations about your growth. These setbacks can be especially crushing because they are of your own design.

One example of this would be setting too low a budget for something like advertising. You might think early on that you only need word of mouth to get you going, and then realize later that you actually need to advertise, but find that it just isn't in the budget. This can then cause you to overhaul your entire business's budget, meaning that other things will have to suffer. In the end, it might end up costing you more money and even some time that could otherwise have been potentially profitable. For new entrepreneurs, it's often those initial mistakes that can end up costing big time in the long run.

How to Fix It

The best way to avoid these business plan mistakes is to simply spend as much time as you can on the planning stage. Do not rush the planning. Yes, you are probably very anxious to get started on your business, but it can be absolutely crucial to your future success. So, spending those extra few hours ironing out every snag in your business plan could potentially save you a lot of time and money. Another great thing you can do to make sure your business plan is solid before you start is to show it to someone else, preferably someone who has had entrepreneurial experience in the past. A fresh pair of eyes can really be very enlightening for your business plan. Chances are, when you have another person look it over, especially if it's someone with experience, that other person is going to point out something that you didn't notice at first. This little detail could potentially save you a lot of money down the road. So, before you actually start your business for real, consider getting someone else to look at your plan, or at least just look at it extra carefully yourself a few times, to avoid any of those pesky setbacks.

LACK OF MARKET KNOWLEDGE

Knowing the market you are trying to enter is absolutely essential for any aspiring entrepreneur. If you are going to be working within a market, you should make sure that you know it inside and out. Big corporations understand this. They pay millions of dollars on market research, funding things like demographic studies, focus groups, and pilot projects. Obviously, as a young startup entrepreneur, you can't afford to do these things, but you can try your best to do versions of them. This kind of research can do wonders for your business, turning it from an idea that only exists in your head to something that has real-world potential. Here are some great suggestions for how you can conduct low-stakes and low-cost market research as an upstart entrepreneur.

Method #1: Friend Focus Groups

As a teenager, you probably don't have access to the kinds of paid, professional focus groups that big companies have access to. But you likely have a circle of friends and acquaintances at school or through extracurriculars that might be willing to test out your products or services. Many other teens, especially if they are your friends, might be happy to help you out for a slice of pizza, a free product, or even a small amount of cash like $5 or $10. Try inviting a group of friends over, offering them your product, and asking for their honest opinion. If you want them to be honest, you could even have everyone write down what they think anonymously and submit it to you in an envelope, that way no one has to worry about your feelings.

Of course, you should tailor the focus group to your projected customers. Generally, you should try to find people as close to your intended ideal customer as possible. At the very least, you should find people in the right age group, since this is one of the most important indicators of someone's potential as a customer. If you are intending to sell to people at your school, then using your friends is great because even if they don't go to your school, they are of a similar age and likely have similar interests and life situations. If you want to start a lawn care business, however, then you should try to find people who own homes with lawns, possibly some of your neighbors or parents' friends. Tailoring your research to the kind of person that you want to sell to is essential to create a strong and sustainable market research base and really understand what your customers like.

Method #2: Surveys

If you want to get a wider sample of feedback, then you can create some surveys. Surveys are great because, unlike a focus group, they standardize the feedback with specific questions and don't require you to provide the product or service to everyone that you survey. You can post a Google form on your social media and ask friends to fill it out. You can even offer an incentive, like entering them into a draw to win a gift card or a free product or service if they fill it out. This kind of market research is somewhat less precise and in-depth than an actual focus group, since the questions will be more generic. It will also be highly hypothetical, since you will be surveying a group of people who haven't used your product. For this reason, your results will be based on what the surveyed group thinks about the *idea* of your business, not the product.

This might work well for the premise, rather than the quality of the actual product. For example, surveying people about whether they are interested in custom-made vegan cupcakes will be effective for analyzing demand for that product, but it won't be able to evaluate whether your cupcakes actually taste good. Therefore, when you are doing this research, bear in mind that the quality of your actual product will make a difference in whether or not your focus group actually likes what you are selling.

Method #3: Research the History of Similar Companies

You can learn a lot by looking into the successes of other companies that have started in the same place as you. Look at some of your favorite entrepreneurs and see what you can find out from them. See if you can find out how they started their company, what kind of markets they started with, and how they scaled up. This is actually some of the best market research you can do because you can watch someone else build their business from the ground up. Doing this kind of role-model-based research will also help you to see what kinds of markets you should be trying to corner during different stages of your business, which is extremely valuable information.

COMPETITION

Obviously, competition is a huge barrier to most businesses. You know the big ones, Coke versus Pepsi, McDonald's versus Burger King, Apple versus Microsoft. But your local area is most likely going to have other companies attempting to corner the same markets that you are. This isn't necessarily a bad thing, but it does mean that you are going to have to do something to differentiate yourself. Unless you are very lucky, and you are actually the first person in your area to think of it, you are definitely going to encounter people doing the same thing as you. So, here, we are going to list for you some of the best ways that you can set yourself apart from the crowd and assert yourself as the best among your competition.

Strategy #1: Distinctive Branding

One of the most genius aspects of Apple's marketing is that they have such a clear, distinctive brand. They have achieved this through many different avenues over the years. One of the most memorable is their distinctive white earbuds. These white wires featured heavily in their marketing during the early stages of the iPod. This was so distinctive because so many headphone wires were gray or black at the time, meaning that if you had an iPod, everyone could immediately tell. Thus, they were able to stick out from the crowd and really corner those extra markets to help ward off the competition. You could also use something similar, such as a distinctive logo or brand color. Implementing something very distinctive can help you to differentiate your brand and help people remember you better than your competition.

Strategy #2: Undercutting Price

The easiest way, of course, to divert attention away from your competition is to offer a lower price for the same service. This is generally frowned upon, but there are several reasons why it can be okay. First of all, there is a strong likelihood that you are less experienced than the competition. If you are offering the same service, it is only natural that you would offer a lower price, since you are going to have fewer resources and less expertise. Some customers might still stick with your competition because they have developed a strong trust with them, or they want someone who's more experienced. Thus, you are not necessarily going to position yourself as an undercutter to your competition, but merely a less experienced option at a lower price. You lowering your prices is then seen as leveling the playing field. So, if you have a lot of experienced competitors in your area, you should consider charging less so that you can compete with them.

Strategy #3: Put Your Personality First

At the beginning of your business's journey, your most valuable asset is actually you. Your personality and distinctive qualities as an entrepreneur are paramount to making sure you get into the right place with your business. If you hide these qualities, then people won't know who you really are or get to trust your business through your personality. Putting your business's qualities first is great, but if it's a very new business, people won't be sure that they can trust you, so make sure that you come across as trustworthy and charismatic. This is one of the best ways to stand out from the crowd because you are using your own unique qualities. People will remember you, not necessarily your business. So, make sure to let your uniqueness shine and put that at the forefront.

ACCIDENTALLY BREAKING LAWS

As a young person, it's really hard to know all the laws of your country and area. Chances are, you haven't even filed your own taxes before, so paperwork and administrative tasks can be really daunting. As a result, there are several laws that are really easy to break as a young entrepreneur. Luckily, none of them have insanely serious consequences, so you will certainly be able to figure them out. However, many come with financial setbacks like fines, which you never want to have in the early stages of your business. Refer back to some of the most important laws that we talked about back in Chapter 5 and make sure that you are meeting all your local requirements. The general rules you should be the most concerned about are taxation, licensing, and copyright. Ensuring that you don't break any of these laws will mean you can avoid having any suspensions to your business or paying any exorbitant fines. If you make sure of this, you will have smooth sailings going forward.

TAKING LONG BREAKS

Running a business is all about consistency. Businesses run on customers remembering who you are and relying on the ability to purchase your product or service whenever they want. Have you ever had a favorite shop that had limited or irregular hours? It can be really frustrating when you want to shop there, but they never seem to be open. If you take long breaks or have your product unavailable for long periods of time, then you run the risk of losing your loyal customer base.

Because loyal customers take a lot of work to attain, you never want to put that valuable asset in jeopardy. For this reason, when you decide to start your business, you should be able to solidly commit to a consistent output. Make sure that for at least the next year, you are going to be available to your customers at consistent hours. You shouldn't take too much time off, especially without warning, and you should make sure that your stock and your services are always in good supply, so you don't gain a reputation for being consistently sold out. Taking breaks is, of course, healthy, but it can also be detrimental to your business, especially in the first year when you are going to be scaling up all the time and establishing those strong customer relationships. Here, we will show you some great tips for handling downtime as a beginner entrepreneur.

Tip #1: Take Smaller Breaks

Burning out is obviously a huge risk as an entrepreneur. Thus, you want to make sure that you aren't overworking yourself or putting yourself through too much stress. So, how do you balance getting proper rest with maintaining availability to your customers? Well, the key is to take more frequent, smaller breaks. Let me explain what I mean. It is much better to take two or three days off every week than to take a week off every month, or a month off every year. This week or month can completely throw off your business model. If you are a business that runs on necessities, such as lawn or pet care, then your customers might actually seek those services elsewhere, meaning you could potentially permanently lose a customer. If you don't run on necessities, they might simply forget you exist and stop purchasing from you. Taking long breaks will mean you run the risk of losing customers. Thus, you should take fewer, smaller breaks to keep your foot in the door with all your customers while avoiding burnout.

Tip #2: Take Consistent Breaks

The other major factor you need to consider is consistency. If a business is unavailable or closed on the same day every week, you can remember and plan around that. But if they are closed on random days, then you can never know for sure whether you are going to be able to go there on any given day. Thus, it's always more customer-forward to plan any days off and be very consistent about them. So, you could make it clear on your website that you are never available on Mondays and Tuesdays, or that you only work on weekends. That way, your customers have a reliable time that they can always contact you. Thus, you know you are not going to lose customers over frustrations to do with your unavailability.

Tip #3: Give Lots of Warning

If you do need to take a break that is not in your regular time-off schedule, say, to go on a trip or something, then you should make sure to give as much warning as possible. Post on all your social media and even let each customer know personally if you perform a regular service. It can be especially customer-forward to even arrange temporary coverage for customers while you are gone. This will show them you really care about service and will also prevent another company from swooping in before you come back.

For example, if you run a dog-walking company, ask a friend to cover your dog walks for you while you are gone so that your customers don't arrange permanent services with another company. If you provide a product, this warning can also help your customers get their orders in on time if they want something for while you are gone. For example, if you run a jewelry business and are going to take August off, but one of your customers wants to gift one of your pieces to someone with an August birthday, they will be able to order their jewelry ahead of time. You can even make a cutoff date, saying, for example, all orders made by July 20th are guaranteed to be filled by the time you take your break. This way, no customer gets left behind, and everyone can make their arrangements around your time off. Being transparent helps customers feel taken care of and will assure none of them are left in the lurch because of your break.

BURNOUT

That being said, burnout is also a big problem for entrepreneurs. Yes, you should avoid taking too many breaks and you should be working as hard as you can, but you should also make sure you are not heading toward burnout. Burnout might not sound that bad, but many recent studies are exploring how harmful and counterproductive it can actually be in the long run. Burnout isn't just becoming tired from too much work, it is actually a medical condition that can cause you to lose years of productivity. Many people are realizing that it can take months or years to fully recover from burnout, meaning you are going to lose that valuable time off of your business. If you are determined to become a successful teen entrepreneur, then you should make sure that you are actually taking burnout very seriously. Here are some important tips for how to avoid this dangerous condition.

Tip #1: Check in With Yourself

Being an entrepreneur requires a lot of deep self-knowledge. You will need to fully examine everything you are doing and understand when it is too much for you. Part of this is knowing how to properly check in with yourself. Being able to listen to your body and know when it is telling you to stop is imperative. If you start to notice that you are not finishing things in time or you are feeling tired and stressed all the time, then you might need to scale your business back. Chances are, these feelings are the early warning signs of burnout, which, if not dealt with properly, can lead to your business stopping dead in its tracks. To make sure your business stays afloat, sometimes that means taking a step back and only doing what is possible for you. This way, you can keep your business going and maintain your mental health.

Tip #2: Outsource Some Things

Sometimes, you realize you need to scale back, but you have already made a bunch of commitments to your customers. This is a huge problem, since you never want to disappoint anyone or produce rushed work. Therefore, you need to find a way to take a step back without necessarily causing setbacks to your business. One of the best ways to do this is to outsource some of your work. Consider hiring someone to help you with parts of the process, even if it's just behind-the-scenes administrative tasks. Having someone handle these things for you is a huge weight off your mind and can help you focus more intensely on the creative parts of the process. There's no shame in asking for help, so to avoid burnout, don't be afraid to outsource some of your more arduous tasks.

Tip #3: Prioritize Sustainability

In general, it is better to get into a slower, more sustainable cycle of work than the overworking and crashing cycle. Overworking cycles essentially consist of you working yourself until you burn out, crashing hard until you are rested, then starting the cycle again. This pattern is incredibly unhealthy, leading to lots of stress and probably long periods of low or nonexistent productivity. Sustainability, on the other hand, means that you are working at a more consistent, sustainable rate, making sure that you are never overworking. This will avoid the crash cycle and ensure that you will always have a consistent output. It's a much healthier lifestyle and will mean that your business will probably last longer. So, you should only take on tasks that you know you can complete and allow yourself some breathing room.

GAP BETWEEN KNOWLEDGE AND SKILLS

Many people have great skills that they can put on display in the marketplace, but having the knowledge to really apply those skills is something altogether. For example, you might be a great pianist, but knowing how to market yourself as a great session musician or lobby player is a completely different matter.

Being an entrepreneur is about so much more than just having a great product or service. It is being a jack-of-all-trades: a marketing executive, accountant, salesperson, and business planner all wrapped in one. These skills are not easy to acquire and take a lot of learning and trial and error to achieve. One of the biggest mistakes early entrepreneurs make is taking skills for granted and not bothering to upskill in these areas. They might think: *I have a great product—it should sell itself*. But in reality, a great product can go overlooked if it doesn't have a solid team behind it. If you don't work hard at the business side of things, your skills will likely go unnoticed, so make sure you train as hard at entrepreneurship as you train at your craft. After that, you can let your talents speak for themselves.

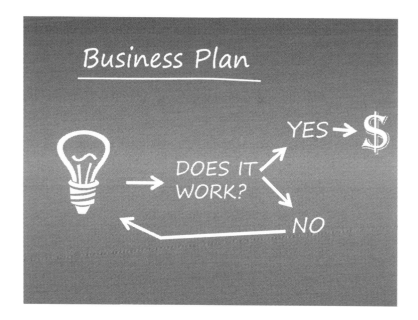

UNREALISTIC EXPECTATIONS

And finally, one of the biggest sources of discouragement for young entrepreneurs is simply having expectations that are too high for what you can actually, reasonably achieve. You need to learn one of these two things: to have realistic expectations or to keep going in the face of failure. If you internalize just one of these, you will go far. Having realistic expectations is a great place to start because they will help you to understand how far you should reasonably be able to go in a short period of time. This doesn't mean you lack ambition; it simply means that you're not asking more of yourself than you can actually give.

In the long run, realistic expectations can really help your self-esteem and your rational evaluation of your business, making you a more mature and grounded entrepreneur. But say you're different, say you're someone who loves having crazy ambitious ideas. That's great! You will likely experience a lot of disappointment, but if you can turn that disappointment and failure into more ambition, then you will go far. It's the people who get too discouraged when their endeavors don't meet their expectations that end up quitting too early. Thus, it's not so much about the realism of your expectations, but more the relationship between those expectations and your motivation. If your expectations are causing you to constantly feel disappointed with yourself and you want to quit, then you should probably change them. But if your expectations are helping you soar far beyond what you thought you could do, then you're on the right track! Just make sure you are always looking ahead and not getting discouraged.

8

LOOK UP

By now, you should have a pretty good idea of what it's like to be an entrepreneur and start your own business. But one nagging question may be occupying you: Why me? Why a young teenager with no experience at all? How do I know that I'm going to be able to make it? Well, it's important to understand two things. Number one, all the greats had to start somewhere. There was a point in time when even your biggest entrepreneurial heroes were beginners just like yourself. And number two: There are plenty of teen entrepreneurs out there who have hit it big at your age.

There's nothing stopping you from going from the least experienced entrepreneur to someone who dominates the entrepreneurial scene in your community. All it takes is drive, a great idea, and a little inspiration. In this chapter, we are going to focus on the inspirational side of things, helping you to see all the potential in yourself through the success stories of others. We will lead you through the success stories of 10 different teen entrepreneurs who were able to make it before age 20. These stories should show you that you don't have to be middle aged to be a great entrepreneur and that you too can start experiencing success as soon as possible!

ASHLEY QUALLS

Way back in 2004, Ashley was just an ordinary freshman in high school. She had a MySpace account, like many other teens, but instead of using it to waste time, she decided to put the platform to good use. One of the coolest things about MySpace was that you could make custom layouts. But not everyone is a great designer, and many teens struggled to design layouts that really fit with their personalities. Ashley, however, was a great designer. She was able to see what people wanted and take it to the next level. She had a vision that she would start to custom design people's MySpace pages for them, helping them to really express their personalities. She started Whateverlife.com, which was a free service made possible by ad layouts. This was a great idea, since there was no barrier for her customers to give it a try. It's a lot easier to sell something when it's free. In just a few years, she was getting millions of dollars in revenue, becoming a millionaire before she was 20! Her story is particularly inspirational to teens looking to make money from the internet. In the early days of the profitable web, she really proved that you could make a career through the net and helped pioneer a whole industry. If you are looking to get into anything to do with design or tech, then you should absolutely look up to Ashley Qualls and consider her work as a prime example of that kind of career trajectory.

JULIETTE BRINDAK

Another creative person who was able to turn their talents into big bucks, Juliette Brindak is an artist, web designer, and entrepreneur. She was only 16 years old when she founded her website *Miss O and Friends*, an online gaming platform aimed at teenage girls. She based the website on her own unique art style, which she began developing when she was just 10 years old. She started creating cartoon characters based on her and her sister, then eventually for her wider circle of friends. People always loved her creations and wanted her to draw characters based on them. She started the website to meet this demand, naming it after her sister Olivia ("Miss O") and launching to huge success. Her site was also powered by ad revenue, making her free service infinitely profitable to her. Another great entrepreneur who made it before 20, Juliette shows that having a creative spirit can also lead to being an exceptional entrepreneur.

SEAN BELNIK

Many teens love collecting things—action figures, trading cards, comic books—but did you know that you can actually make a career from collecting and trading? Sean Belnik started just like any other 16-year-old card collector, but he had an edge. He started an online business selling his trading cards. Through flipping cards that he knew to be valuable, he was able to build a strong business. He then was able to extend outward from playing cards and into other things like furniture. He founded BizChair.com, which is a multi-million-dollar furniture selling website. As we can see, there sure is a theme with online selling and teen entrepreneurs. Teens definitely have an edge over adults in this way, able to adopt trends and expand into new markets much faster than a lot of adults. Case in point: Sean was worth $24 million by the time he turned 20, proving that age really is just a number when it comes to being an entrepreneur.

JOHN KOON

At 16 years old, John Koon had a vision. He was very knowledgeable in the auto parts space, but he knew that he could do more than just work as a mechanic. He was able to see the potential growth in the industry of selling auto parts, and thus, founded the famous business Extreme Performance Motorsports in New York City. This business quickly grew to be super successful. In a short amount of time, he was already being offered a gig providing parts to reality TV shows on MTV. Talk about a teenager's dream! From there, his stardom only grew. He was able to partner with the artist Jeezy to create their own joint fashion line. Being on TV and designing fashion with rappers... It doesn't get much better than that! As you can probably imagine, John is now worth over $40 million and is projected to become a billionaire in the coming years. Through his determination, he proved that a small passion can turn into something truly enormous.

DAVID AND CATHERINE COOK

As a brother and sister team, David and Catherine Cook were whizzes of the social media scene. They understood the value of social media as a means of creating memories and documenting your experiences.

But they also understood how under-curated platforms like Instagram and Facebook could be, with all your photos scattered on the same platform and not much opportunity for sorting. That's why they created MyYearbook.com, a website designed for teens to be able to create their own digital yearbooks. It was brilliant because they could customize their yearbooks to be about them and their friends. It's basically a curated social media feed meets high school yearbook, which works together to create the perfect time capsule to remember the best years of your life. They managed to convince their other brother to invest in their idea and have hit it big, with the website being worth around $100 million today.

TYLER DIKMAN

Sometimes, those years you spend tinkering around on a computer in your bedroom pay off. Tyler Dikman developed a keen eye for fixing computers from a young age. At a very young age, he realized how profitable this enterprise could really be and so he began charging for his services, making around $15 an hour at only 13 years old! But his entrepreneurial journey didn't end there. Tyler was quickly noticed by investment giant Merrill Lynch who hired him at age 15. This is completely unprecedented for a person of that age and really launched Tyler into stardom. After this gig taught him the ins and outs of the industry, he was able to start his own business and make it a resounding success. The business, Cooltronics, specialized in repairing computers. From there, he was able to make millions and was even featured on the 25 Under 25 list from Businessweek. Now, that's a list that you want to get on!

FRASER DOHERTY

Moving into the culinary side of things, Fraser Doherty was able to make his fortune using the simplest thing in the world: a jam recipe. Only 14, he was able to recognize that his grandmother had truly one of the best jams out there. The Scottish teen quickly learned how to replicate it and the profits started rolling in. He founded a business, calling it SuperJam. By the time he was 16, that business was booming. His real big break happened when a major UK grocery store started carrying his jams. Almost overnight, he was officially a millionaire. Fraser's story shows you that truly anything can be turned into a profitable business, even something as simple as a jar of jam.

MARK ZUCKERBURG

Yes, you read that correctly. Mark Zuckerburg was actually a teen entrepreneur. He founded Facebook while he was still in college, making him one of the youngest starters among contemporary billionaires today. You can see how he was similar to other teens in tech, like Juliette Brindak or Tyler Dikman. These teenagers were able to corner a market that adults were still slowly catching onto. By capitalizing on their new knowledge, they were able to really corner a market that might not have been cornered otherwise. We can see how Mark starting Facebook was a very similar journey. He saw a gap in the scene, in this case early social media, and was able to fill it with his visionary ideas. Today, he is worth over $20 billion, showing that even a young upstart entrepreneur can end up among the greats.

JOHN MAGENNIS

Speaking of web design, John Magennis was one of the youngest tech innovators. At just 14, he was able to teach himself how to make stellar websites for his clients. He started out charging just $15 per site. But everyone who got in at this stage is probably very thankful, since John now charges up to $30,000 for his sites. He was able to grow so quickly because of the sheer quality of the product he was offering. He was so successful that he actually hit a million dollars in earnings by the time he turned 16 years old. Not bad for someone who hasn't even finished high school yet! People like John really prove that it doesn't matter who you are, you can find success with the right amount of determination.

KIOWA KAVOVIT

As the youngest person on this list (and, incidentally, the youngest person to ever feature on *Shark Tank*), Kiowa Kavovit is an inspiration to all. She had a simple idea: bandages that paint onto the cut instead of being pasted on. She dubbed her invention "Boo Boo Goo," and really hit the ground running. At just six years old, she pitched her invention to the Sharks. They were so impressed that she earned an investment of $100,000.

Her company only grew from there. She became a millionaire in 2014 from her design. So, if you ever feel like you're too young to start putting yourself out there as an entrepreneur, just remember Kiowa's story and know that she was pounding the pavement when she was barely out of kindergarten. If she can do it, then you can too!

OVERVIEW

All these teens have one thing in common: perseverance. Many kids and teens have ideas for businesses. You'll see plenty of young people with things like lemonade stands and bracelet-making businesses. But what separates them from the kids above who were able to take their home-spun businesses and turn them into something truly extraordinary? What made their businesses take off while others remained simple dreams of childhood to be abandoned? Well, it was perseverance, first and foremost. The teens you have seen on this list weren't just kids with ideas, or even great ideas, they were teens who had the vision to turn their ideas into something more.

When they were selling small websites or providing small services for people, they were looking ahead. They were able to see past the everyday and pursue something that was completely new. They could strip away all the excess to see where success really lies. And this is what you will need to do to get your name among them. Not only will your business idea have to be extraordinary, but it will also have to make a difference in the world and soar past what others might expect of you. You will need the perseverance to turn that dream into a reality.

So, what are some ways you can do this? What are the actual qualities of personality that build this perseverance? Those are great questions. It takes more than just sticking to your guns to make an excellent entrepreneur. Here, we will look at some of the skills these teens have that you should try to add to your roster.

Skill #1: An Eye for Gaps

Another teen entrepreneur we didn't discuss on the list, Nick D'Aloisio, credits much of his success to his ability to recognize gaps in the market. Gaps in the market are essentially empty spaces in an industry, a lack of some necessary product or service someone might need. A non-visionary might not be able to see or think of any gaps in the market. They might look at all the products and services available in the world and think: What else could there be? But a visionary has the ability to look at these things and see exactly what's missing.

Maybe it's a unique way of delivering a certain service, or a more efficient way of doing so. Maybe it's a product that you know people would use but it isn't available to them yet. Or maybe it's even your own creative ideas that you want to share with the world. Whatever the gap is, that's what will make your product not only unique but necessary. People won't just want your product because they haven't seen it before, they will want it because it meets an unmet need in their life that they didn't even know was there. If you are the kind of person who can see gaps in the market, like many of the teens on the above list, then you will go very far in life.

Skill #2: A Hardworking Spirit

Throughout this book, we've talked a lot about working "smart, not hard," and how you know when you need to take a break, and all that. But at the end of the day, it is very simple: The business people who work hard are able to achieve their dreams, and the ones who don't simply don't make it. All of the teens on this list are the kind of people who rise to challenges, who keep working even though there might be other things they are more interested in doing, and who keep on keeping on even when the going gets tough. That is how they were able to turn their small side hustles into multimillion-dollar companies. The continued drive allowed them to keep working through all the challenges and even monotony at times. This is one of the most important qualities that you will need to embody if you are going to make it like all these other teens made it.

Skill #3: Modesty

If you've ever been to a theater audition, then you will know that there is quite often a direct correlation between the amount of arrogance someone has and their talent. Often, the person who gets up there, eager to impress, is low on talent, while the shy person hiding in the corner comes out with a golden voice. Now, of course confidence is important, but there is a fine line between confidence and arrogance. You can be confident and modest at the same time. As a businessperson, you should never be arrogant enough to assume that someone wants to work with you or that they want to buy your product. You should be confident enough to know that what you're selling is good, but modest enough to respect your customers and remember that you still have to sell to them. If you are able to do this, then you will have a much easier time selling to people and constructing your brand. Follow these skills, and you will be able to take your business to the level that these teens before you have done.

NOW IS THE TIME FOR PERSONAL GROWTH, SELF-MOTIVATION, AND FINANCIAL CONTROL

With the right information and a solid plan, you have all you need to stay ahead of the game and turn those dreams into reality. If I could ask just one thing from you, it would be to leave a review on Amazon and help other teens do the same.

IN UNDER 1 MINUTE
YOU CAN HELP OTHERS JUST LIKE YOU BY LEAVING A REVIEW!

There is no doubt that your generation is going to make waves in the future. The more teen millionaire entrepreneurs in the world, the more you can achieve together! Thank you so much for your review in advance and good luck with your financial freedom!

CONCLUSION

So, you've made it to the end. You've read through all the advice we have to give about starting your own business as a teen. You've learned some of the most valuable insider business knowledge there is to give, and you have seen the process of starting a business up close. Let's have a little overview of what you've learned and summarize some of the key takeaways from this book.

In Chapter 1, we talked all about general money skills. While you were reading, you might have been thinking: *What is the point of this? I want to be an entrepreneur!* But, hopefully, now you understand how important these initial skills were to discuss. You now understand the value of personal financial skills as they relate to business skills. You know that what you do with your personal finances affects what you do with your professional finances. In that chapter, you learned how to manage money effectively for yourself and your business.

In Chapter 2, we then moved on to the purpose of starting a business. We discussed the importance of passion as it relates to being a businessperson and we stressed that you should always make sure you do the things you love. We also talked about the charitable and impact-focused side to being a businessperson, arguing that if your business makes a difference to the world and society, it will be much more fulfilling for you in the long run. In that chapter, you learned the building blocks for what motivates you as a businessperson.

In Chapter 3, we talked about the importance of your skills. We discussed how to discover your existing skills and how to build new skills. We discussed the relationship between strength and weakness as a businessperson and in your personal life as well. And most of all, we talked about how doing what you are good at can really help personalize your business and its brand. In that chapter, you learned how to harness your skills and put them to good use in your business.

In Chapter 4, we talked about how to discover your niche as a businessperson. This chapter dealt with the ways to corner particular markets and score customers for yourself while dealing with competition. In that chapter, you learned how to harness the uniqueness of your company and target the customers who would respond to that uniqueness.

In Chapter 5, we really got into the nitty-gritty details of starting a business. We gave you a step-by-step guide to building your business from the ground up and helped you through some of the administrative tasks that tend to be more intimidating to teens. In that chapter, you really got to see the process of starting a business from a realistic perspective.

In Chapter 6, we talked about the importance of upskilling and harnessing your most important skills. We zeroed in on a few skills that are particularly important to a business person and gave you some tips on how to get there. In that chapter, you learned the virtues of the entrepreneur and how to follow those values.

In Chapter 7, we took a turn toward some of the negative things that can happen as an entrepreneur. This was to warn you about some of the issues that could arise in the coming years, and also to give you some strategies on how to overcome those things. In that chapter, you learned to be prepared for the worst and always have a solution up your sleeve.

And finally, in Chapter 8, we inspired you with the stories of some of the world's greatest teen entrepreneurs. These teens demonstrate some truly admirable qualities that are integral for any young entrepreneur to embody. In that chapter, you learned that everything is possible.

Hopefully, this book has been eye-opening, inspiring, and engrossing all at once. We hope it has made you excited to finally get out there and start your business. If you enjoyed the book or learned anything from it, we would very much appreciate a review. Who knows? Maybe you will achieve all your dreams and that review will become very valuable one day. But whatever happens, remember to work hard, keep a keen, visionary mindset, and always have your eye on the prize!

GLOSSARY

Accountant: A person with expertise in filing taxes who can help you sort out your business finances.

Audit: When the government performs an in-depth spot-check of your taxes, ensuring that you have followed all the rules and paid the taxes you owe.

Budget: The strategy of allocating specific amounts of money to different areas to make sure you are spending properly.

Credit rating or score: A score evaluating how efficiently you pay off debts such as student loans, credit cards, and mortgages.

Evaluation: A calculation you make about the value of your company, usually based on existing or projected sales and assets.

Financial freedom: The ability to make passive income off of your business without having to work anymore.

Investment: Putting money toward a company with the promise of receiving a percentage of profits in the long run.

Negotiation: Going back and forth about deals, each person trying to achieve a compromise.

Outsourcing: Hiring someone else to do the work that you don't have the skills or time to do.

Overhead: Money that has to go toward expenses for your business such as rent, materials, advertising, etc.

Passive income: Income that comes from investments or business profits, meaning that you don't have to work to receive their income.

Profit: The amount of money you make after you subtract your overhead.

Revenue: The gross amount of money you make from your company before subtracting overhead.

Savings account: A type of bank account that generates revenue through light investments.

Startup costs: The amount of money you need to spend on supplies, equipment, permits, etc. before you start your company.

Tax write-off: An expense for your business that you can subtract from your taxable income.

REFERENCES

Alton, L. (2017, May 24). *What young entrepreneurs can learn from the success of their peers*. Entrepreneur. https://www.entrepreneur.com/leadership/what-young-entrepreneurs-can-learn-from-the-success-of/294452

Alton, L. (2016, December 28). *How to turn your hobby into a profitable business venture*. Entrepreneur. https://www.entrepreneur.com/business-news/how-to-turn-your-hobby-into-a-profitable-business-venture/286813

Bennett, R. (n.d.). *6 top reasons to save your money*. Bankrate. https://www.bankrate.com/banking/savings/top-reasons-to-save-money/

Bester, A. (2022, April 12). *Start your business: 7 reasons to work for yourself*. GetSmarter Blog. https://www.getsmarter.com/blog/career-advice/start-your-business-7-reasons-to-work-for-yourself/

Boitnott, J. (n.d.). *40 young people who became millionaires by 20*. Inc. Retrieved September 22, 2014, from https://www.inc.com/john-boitnott/40-young-people-who-became-millionaires-before-they-were-20.html

Business quotes that will unlock your true potential. (n.d.). Quotlr. Retrieved February 26, 2023, from https://quotlr.com/quotes-about-starting-a-business

Cooks-Campbell, A. (2022, July 11). *The importance of knowing yourself: Your key to fulfillment*. Better Up. https://www.betterup.com/blog/the-importance-of-knowing-yourself

Creating a budget with a personal budget spreadsheet. (2019). Better Money Habits. https://bettermoneyhabits.bankofamerica.com/en/saving-budgeting/creating-a-budget

Determining your business's market value. (n.d.). The Hartford. https://www.thchartford.com/business-insurance/strategy/selling-a-business/determining-market-value

11 small business ideas for teens in 2023. (n.d.). Shopify. Retrieved

February 26, 2023, from https://www.shopify.com/za/blog/busi
ness-ideas-for-teens

Ellin, B. (2020, April 2). *The legal requirements for starting a business.*
Y&NY Growth Hub. https://www.ynygrowthhub.com/blog/arti
cle/what-are-the-legal-requirements-for-starting-a-business/

Ellis, K. (2022, September 7). *Teenage money management: 8 ways to teach
your teen.* Finder. https://www.finder.com/teenage-money-
management

54 ways to save money. (n.d.). America Saves. https://americasaves.org/
resource-center/insights/54-ways-to-save-money/

How can I play music in my business legally? (n.d.). Law Donut. Retrieved
February 26, 2023, from https://www.lawdonut.co.uk/business/
commercial-premises-law/managing-your-premises/how-can-i-
play-music-in-my-business-legally

How much money should I have in order to retire in canada? (n.d.). Dundas
Life. Retrieved February 26, 2023, from https://www.dundaslife.
com/blog/how-much-income-should-i-save

Investing guide for teens (and parents). (n.d.). The Balance. https://www.
thebalancemoney.com/investing-guide-for-teens-and-parents-
4588018

Lake, R. (2022, March 16). *6 types of savings accounts.* Forbes Advisor.
https://www.forbes.com/advisor/banking/savings/types-of-
savings-accounts/

Lilies, M. (2023, January 26). *101 Dave Ramsey quotes that will help you
learn how to become a millionaire.* Parade. https://parade.com/
969637/marynliles/dave-ramsey-quotes/

Matthews, D. (2019, September 15). *Why your business idea is the most
important thing in your startup.* Medium. https://bettermarketing.
pub/why-your-business-idea-is-the-most-important-thing-in-
your-startup-48d0c7728888

Morrison, S. (2022, August 5). *Reasons to do what you love for a living.*
Business News Daily. https://www.businessnewsdaily.com/7995-
reasons-to-do-what-you-love.html

Nast, C. (2017, May 31). *How a 16-year-old girl started a multimillion dollar social network*. Teen Vogue. https://www.teenvogue.com/story/juliette-brindak-hyperlinked-interview

Nickolas, S. (2021, April 30). *Compound interest versus simple interest.* Investopedia. https://www.investopedia.com/ask/answers/042315/what-difference-between-compounding-interest-and-simple-interest.asp

Pablo Picasso. (2009). Henri Matisse. https://www.pablopicasso.org/

Perkins, K. Twitter. https://twitter.com/kendrickperkins/status/1165955901162950657

Porteous, C. (2020, February 25). *8 legal requirements when you start a business.* Entrepreneur. https://www.entrepreneur.com/starting-a-business/8-legal-requirements-when-you-start-a-business/346713

Silver, C. (2022, February 3). *The ultimate guide to financial literacy.* Investopedia. https://www.investopedia.com/guide-to-financial-literacy-4800530

65 niche quotes on success in life. (2021, November 4). Overall Motivation. https://www.overallmotivation.com/quotes/niche-quotes/

Team, T. S. (2022, April 28). *50+ best money mindset quotes for attracting financial success.* The Strive. https://thestrive.co/money-mindset-quotes/

10 quotes on overcoming obstacles that will motivate you. (2021, July 15). Teamphoria. https://www.teamphoria.com/10-quotes-on-overcoming-obstacles-that-will-motivate-you/

10 reasons why teens should start a business. (2015, May 18). Encouraging Moms at Home. https://encouragingmomsathome.com/10-reasons-teens-start-business

10 steps to finding your passion and purpose. (2018, January 24). True Joy Experience. https://www.truejoyexperience.com/10-steps-to-finding-your-passion-and-purpose/

13 inspiring educational quotes for students to help them thrive. (2019, July 2). University of the People. https://www.uopeople.edu/blog/13-inspiring-educational-quotes-for-students-to-help-them-thrive/

Tips for turning your hobby into a career. (n.d.). The Balance. Retrieved

February 26, 2023, from https://www.thebalancemoney.com/how-to-turn-your-hobby-into-a-career-2059663

Top 10 reasons to start your own business. (n.d.). Accion Opportunity Fund. https://aofund.org/resource/top-10-reasons-start-your-own-business/

28 business ideas for teens. (n.d.). NerdWallet. https://www.nerdwallet.com/article/small-business/business-ideas-for-teens

Understanding your money beliefs: Knowledge is power. (n.d.). Aspen Wealth Management. Retrieved February 26, 2023, from https://www.aspenwealthmgmt.com/resource-center/blog/understanding-money-beliefs/

Vincent van Gogh | biography, art, & facts. (2019). In *Encyclopædia Britannica.* https://www.britannica.com/biography/Vincent-van-Gogh

What is a credit score. (n.d.). Equifax. Retrieved February 26, 2023, from https://www.equifax.com/personal/education/credit/score/what-is-a-credit-score/

Wooll, M. (2021, October 19). *Start finding your purpose and unlock your best life.* Better Up. https://www.betterup.com/blog/finding-purpose

IMAGE REFERENCES

Ar130405. (2017). *Success strategy business* [Image]. https://pixabay.com/illustrations/success-strategy-business-solution-2081168/

Aymanajed. (2018). *Laptop office handwriting* [Image]. https://pixabay.com/photos/laptop-office-hand-writing-3196481/

Cytonn. (2018). *Two people shaking hands* [Image]. https://unsplash.com/photos/n95VMLxqM2I

Dumalo, N. (2019). *Person holding visa card and white device* [Image]. https://unsplash.com/photos/lvWw_G8tKsk

GDJ. (2018). *Social media connections networking* [Image]. https://pixabay.com/vectors/social-media-connections-networking-3846597/

Geralt. (2018). *Bulletin board stickies post it* [Image]. https://pixabay.com/photos/bulletin-board-stickies-post-it-3127287/

Geralt. (2015). *Entrepreneur begin startup career* [Image]. https://pixabay.com/photos/entrepreneur-begin-start-up-career-696976/

Jarmoluk. (2014). *Innovation business businessman* [Image]. https://pixabay.com/photos/innovation-business-businessman-561388/

Martin, E. (2017). *Grey concrete building photo* [Image]. https://unsplash.com/photos/2_K82gx9Uk8

Microsoft. (2022). *Free clothing* [Image]. https://unsplash.com/photos/FHhbHW4vFxc

Mohamed_Hassan. (2019). *Financial analysis accounting* [Image]. https://pixabay.com/illustrations/financial-analysis-accounting-4560047/

Nattanan23. (2017). *Money coin investment business* [Image]. https://pixabay.com/photos/money-coin-investment-business-2724241/

PCB-Tech. (2018). *Triangle quality time cost* [Image]. https://pixabay.com/photos/triangle-quality-time-cost-3125882/

Rilsonav. (2016). *Money time is money* [Image]. https://pixabay.com/illustrations/money-time-is-money-1132279/

Smith, I. (2018). *Pen on paper photo* [Image]. https://unsplash.com/photos/AT77Q0Njnt0

Stevepb. (2019). *Income tax calculator accounting* [Image]. https://pixabay.com/photos/income-tax-calculator-accounting-4097292/

Tumisu. (2018). *Analytics charts business woman* [Image]. https://pixabay.com/photos/analytics-charts-business-woman-3265840/

Tumisu. (2015). *Business plan startup strategy* [Image]. https://pixabay.com/illustrations/business-plan-startup-strategy-891339/

Winkler, M. (2020). *Black and silver laptop computer photo* [Image]. https://unsplash.com/photos/IrRbSND5EUc